MALABAR AND THE PORTUGUESE

MALABAR AND THE PORTUGUESE

Being a History of the Relations of the Portuguese with Malabar from 1500 to 1663

BY

K. M. PANIKKAR, B.A. (OXON.)

FOREWORD

BY

Lieut.-Col. Sir Richard Carnac Temple

GYAN

Published by

GYAN

Gyan Publishing House
5, Ansari Road
Daryaganj, New Delhi-110002
Phone: 011-47034999, 9811692060
E-mail: books@gyanbooks.com

Distribution Network
gyanbooks.com
India, USA, Canada, UK, Australia

ISBN: 978-81-212-8440-0 (HB)
First Published, 1929

2nd Impression 2024

Printed at: Gyan Press, Delhi.

MALABAR AND THE PORTUGUESE
Author: K. M. PANIKKAR

MALABAR AND THE PORTUGUESE

"Mr. Panikkar is the author of excellent historical works. He is a thoughtful author and brings much study to bear upon the subjects which he discusses. His works deserve appreciation for scholarship and research."—*The Hindustan Review.*

"He is a writer of the advanced guard of the best Indian Political thought, who writes with the same respect for other participants in the controversies as he would look for from them, and who forms his conclusions without fear or favour, and states them with frankness and courage."—*The Times of India.*

"Mr. Panikkar is well known as an able and thoughtful writer. He often provokes disagreement, but he is hardly ever unfair; an opponent can always see the reasonableness of his point of view."—*The Times Literary Supplement.*

"He shows considerable skill and analytical acumen."—*The Hindu.*

"He is quite the best writer among Indian publicists. He is candid and his suggestions are therefore always illuminating." — *The Manchester Guardian.*

"He writes from the National standpoint, but he is moderate in tone. He takes a broader view of the situation than writers usually take. We have nothing but praise to offer."—*The Near East and India.*

"He has his own views; but he understands and deals appreciatively with the views of others. He is a master in the art of seeing events as one whole and handles his material with ease."—*The Statesman.*

He writes with commendable moderation."—*The Daily Telegraph.*

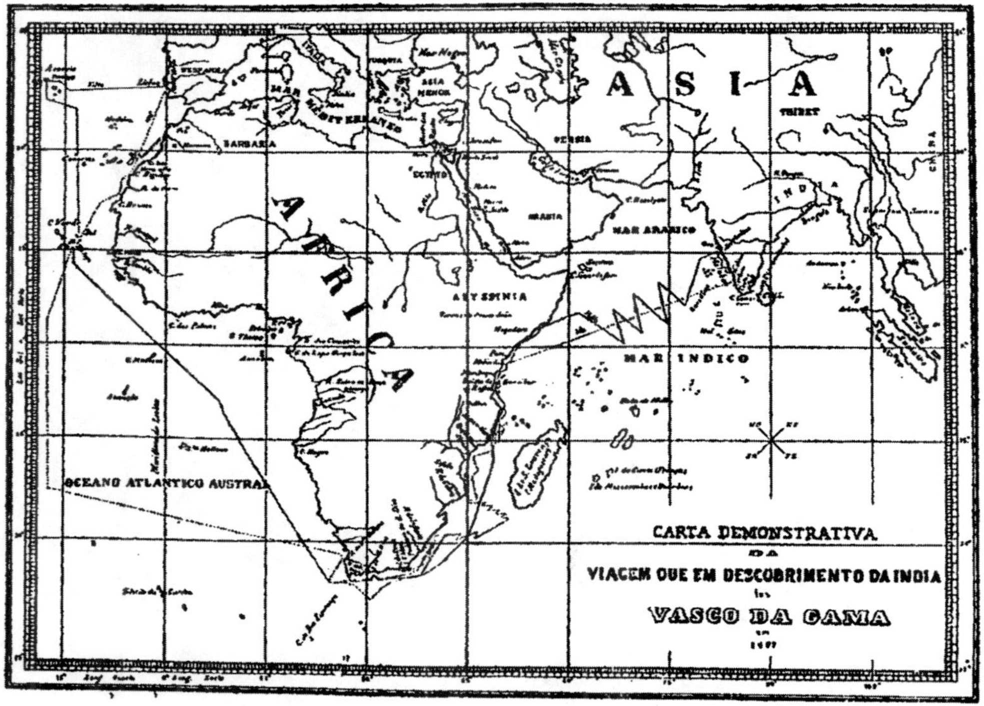

THE ROUTE OF VASCO DA GAMA'S FIRST VOYAGE

MALABAR AND THE PORTUGUESE

Being a History of the Relations of the Portuguese with Malabar from 1500 to 1663

BY

K. M. PANIKKAR, B.A. (Oxon.),

Barrister-at-Law.

DIXON SCHOLAR OF CHRIST CHURCH, OXFORD

Sometime Professor of Modern History, Muslim University, Aligarh.

Author of "The Relations Between the Government of India and the Indian States", "Shri Harsha of Kanauj" Etc.

FOREWORD

BY

Lieut.-Col. Sir Richard Carnac Temple, Bt., C.B., C.I.E.,

F. B. A., F. S. A.,

Hon. Fellow, Trin. Hall, Cambridge

Editor, "The Indian Antiquary"

BOMBAY:

D. B. TARAPOREVALA SONS & Co.

"KITAB MAHAL": HORNBY ROAD

1929

TO

HIS EXCELLENCY

DR. VEIGA SIMOES

MINISTER PLENIPOTENTIARY AND ENVOY EXTRAORDINARY

OF THE PORTUGUESE REPUBLIC,

WHO RENDERED ME INVALUABLE HELP DURING MY STAY

IN PORTUGAL

FOREWORD

Mr. Panikkar has performed a work of value to students in providing a summary of the history of the Portuguese in Malabar. He has, however, thus confined himself to a portion only of their doings in the East, rigorously moreover keeping to this theme, and the chief value of his observations to my mind is that he gives the history from the point of view of the Indian who has been trained in historical research and is capable of bringing out the essentials of the story he has to tell. It is not a pleasant tale, but that is not his fault—rather that of his subject.

He begins by showing how it was possible for the Portuguese to accomplish what they managed to do, as, when Vasco da Gama reached the Malabar Coast the country was split up into petty principalities over whom no one had any real authority—not even the Zamorin of Calicut. So it did not require any particular political insight to play off the princelings along the coast against each other and establish foreign authority over small isolated coastwise areas. Mr. Panikkar has no high opinion of Vasco da Gama and does not class him with the great European explorers. Perhaps he is somewhat hard on him; but, no doubt, Vasco da Gama was not a "great" man in the sense that others of his time and later on were. Mr. Panikkar has indeed but little opinion of any of the Portuguese leaders excepting Albuquerque, Duarte Pacheco as a military luminary, and Affonso Mexia as a financier; and, indeed, these men did some wonderful things, considering the difficulties that surrounded them. He is right also in stating clearly that the Portuguese never had any power or Empire in India, that they never got beyond acquiring a little local authority, strictly confined to small areas around the forts they built along the coast line. Yet, with the fortuitous assistance of general politics in the Near East, and not of their own superior skill, they achieved for a long period their chief object—the destruction of the Egyptian and Venetian trade with the East, and the concentration of it in their own hands on the sea. Some of their Governors saw that it was in sea power only that their chances of success and greatness lay.

In judging of the Portuguese and their actions in India, one has to recollect that they were a century nearer feudal Europe than were any of the other nations that invaded the country—a century further back in civilisation and political organisation. In fact, they had very little of the latter, as practically every Factor had a right to address the Portuguese Crown direct and write home what he thought fit—truth or untruth, praise or slander—of the Viceroy, Governor or other superior authority. Authoritative government is impossible under such conditions, and so the Portuguese officials made it. They destroyed even Albuquerque in the end. One wonders indeed that anything at all was accomplished; and the undoubted fact that trade and civilisation did flourish under them for a time supplies yet another instance, of many in history, of the truth of the dictum that human beings act better than they organise.

In their mediævalism there was little to choose between the higher Portuguese officials and their Indian contemporaries. The insincerity, dishonesty, selfishness, chicanery and cruelty were about on a par, though perhaps, the cruelty of the Portuguese was the greater, and indeed commercial and political intercourse must have been difficult when no man's word was to be trusted on either side. Yet, as aforesaid, they did manage to carry on commerce and the dealings of everyday life. The public proceedings of the Portuguese leaders, great and small, were essentially those of a mediæval people. There was little attempt at straight dealing. It was everyone for himself from the Viceroy downwards, and every kind of official entered into private trade. The strong succeeded in their personal aims; the weak brought disaster on themselves and their following, while, as among all such people, there were individuals who were sufficiently wide-awake to their own interests. Life struggled on; wealth was accumulated in places; extravagant careers were lived through: great houses and towns were built: and there was much show of success. But the whole structure was hollow, and fell before the first equally well-equipped enemy that attacked it. The hollowness was not the result only of the action of the representatives of the Portuguese nation in India. The home government was necessarily ignorant of the conditions, and, as has been already hinted, took the wrong course in ascertaining the truth as to the proceedings of its agents in the East. The entire system showed its inefficiency from the very top. Otherwise such men as Cabral, de Coutinho, Reall, de Meneses, de Sousa and others like them, would not have been sent to high office. The position in India was thus rendered hopeless. Officials were improperly paid, or even not paid at all; the very soldiers were unpaid for a year after arrival in any case; pay counted for little, and perquisites were everything; at first, there was no accounting, and even after it was instituted it was very bad—as a matter of course the currency was soon debased; indeed, selfishness and shortsightedness at home seem to have been endless. At any rate, they led to sending orphan girls to India with appointments—even high ones—as dowries to any husband they might marry on arrival. If such things had not actually happened, one could hardly credit their possibility.

It must not, however, be supposed that no Portuguese showed any of the higher human capacities. The records of Barbosa and Correa, among others, are proof of the contrary. Albuquerque was a real administrator; Duarte Pacheco had considerable military genius, and Affonso Mexia true financial ability as well as honesty of purpose. There were besides, even in the beginning, men who understood; but they were not in supreme power. There were also men who learnt much—more in fact than for a long time did the more successful of the Europeans who followed them to India—of the natives of the country, their tribes, their habits and their religious ideas. An unfortunately bigoted and far too powerful a priesthood led the Portuguese Church in India; but even amongst them there were such true missionaries as Francisco de Xavier. The want of principle, however, in the government and organisation made the situation hopeless. Ignorance in regard to the Indians and their ways was at first complete—so complete indeed that Vasco da Gama and his men at the beginning thought that the Hindu was a kind of Christian. The Mahommedan—the Moor—they knew and hated with a true religious fervour, but Hinduism in any form was a thing unrealised. They soon learnt better; but it will be understood that mistakes were necessarily many, especially as the bigotry never diminished.

Among the mistakes, perhaps the most serious, were that the country could be taken by force, that conversion to the Portuguese form of Christianity of all the Indian population was a feasible proposition, and that the princelings with whom they came in contact were the Princes of India. The pride and self-conceit of the Portuguese, too, were unlimited. They looked on themselves as the salt of the earth, all others being completely below them; and yet they had no repugnance to a mixture of races. Their inferiority in numbers was obvious, and, from the beginning, they sought to set it straight by mixed unions, Portuguese and Indians, not realising that the population resulting would be neither Portuguese nor Indian. The mixture of races thus permitted was carried very far and permeated every class. It unquestionably helped in the fall of the Portuguese as a race in India. At the same time the mixing of European and Indian soldiers and sailors led the way to a most successful organisation, afterwards adopted with a difference by the French and English.

A consideration, like the above, of the conditions of Portuguese power in India, such as it was, explains true tales of the times that otherwise read as pure romances, and there are many such. Take for example the career of Dom Martin (1606-1643). The King of Arakan had a son who was Viceroy of Chittagong, while the Portuguese piratical adventurer, Sebastian Gonsalvez, constituted himself Ruler of the island of Sarandip. The Arakanese Viceroy felt himself uncertain in his post and made overtures to Gonsalvez, who seized the opportunity to better his own position. In the result, a daughter of the Arakanese Viceroy, born of course a Buddhist, was married, as a Christian, to the Portuguese pirate's son. This proceeding was naturally not pleasing to the King of Arakan, who sent his eldest soh to deal with the Viceroy. This eldest son was afterwards a notable King of Arakan and his visit to Chittagong was the end of his brother, the Viceroy; and incidentally, in the sequel, of Gonsalvez also. But the Portuguese priest managed to spirit away two of the Viceroy's children, a boy and a girl, to Hooghly, where they were brought up as Portuguese Christians under the names of Dom Martin and Dona Petronella. It was in accordance with Portuguese manners and policy to treat Dom Martin the Arakanese as a Portuguese gentleman of standing. He, accordingly, served for years as an officer in the Army and Navy in India, and, as it happened, with distinction. Meanwhile his uncle, the King of Arakan, died and his successor was overthrown by a usurper. Portugal also, under John IV, had recently thrown off the Spanish yoke and Dom Martin saw his chance to recover his own throne through Portuguese help. So he managed to get to Portugal, as the first Burmese to visit any European country, in a manner that is romance itself. He obtained an interview with John IV who found him a man of parts and could sympathise with him in his desire to recover his heritage. At any rate, the King equipped an expedition for him, and then, unfortunately, Dom Martin died at sea without even reaching India. So ended, in nothing, an extraordinary romantic career, which might otherwise have seriously affected Burmese history. But the point, in the present connection, is that it was made possible by the conditions of the Portuguese occupation of the Indian coasts. Dom Martin could not have attained the position he achieved under any other European power in India.

Another story of the period, which reads impossible to the modern Englishman, also illustrates the conditions of Portuguese presence in India during the early part of the seventeenth century. Felippe de Brito, a cabin boy and palace menial, rose in three years (1600-1602), during the chaos on the collapse of the Peguan Empire, to the Governorship of Syriam, near Rangoon, for the Arakanese, and finally to the throne of Pegu itself, with a daughter of the Viceroy of Goa for wife. Like other Portuguese of the time, he was an aggressive, headstrong man, with no idea of ingratiating himself to his people or neighbours. So in 1613 he was ousted and impaled alive, while his unfortunate queen, who seems to have been a typically proud Portuguese woman, was sent as a slave to Ava. Here again we can see that it was the condition of Portuguese administration in India and the East that made such a story possible. There are others equally astonishing.

The mention of Sebastian Gonsalvez, who may be looked on as a real pirate, induces me to remark on what is usually called piracy in the Indian seas in the sixteenth and seventeenth centuries. The Portuguese admitted the right of other European nations to the freedom of the Western oceans, but claimed, under

Papal authority, to be the only lawful sailors on those in the East. Under such a claim, sailors of all other nations, using them without Portuguese permission, were pirates. This is why the Kunjali Marakkars were looked on as such, though they were in reality the admirals of the Zamorin of Calicut. They fought the Portuguese with varying success for a hundred years until they became overgrown subjects of their nominal master and were destroyed by the Portuguese through his connivance. So was every "Moor", and the commander of every ship of another European nation sailing in the East, a pirate in Portuguese eyes. In one sense indeed every ship, Portuguese or other, capable of fighting, as were most of the large vessels in the Eastern seas, was in those days a pirate craft.

Although the Portuguese invasion of the Indian coastal regions was, in the light of the above observations, only an incident in the general history of the country, it had a profound effect on Malabar. The tendency of the rule of the native princelings was towards a consolidation of power in one of them, the Zamorin of Calicut, and there can be little doubt but that something of the kind would have been the fate of Malabar had it not been for the disruptive effect of the intervention of the Portuguese. Their action prevented any such event taking place, and after the fall of their influence nothing of the kind was possible. In fact, the present condition of Malabar under British rule is largely the result of Portuguese action. Again, as has been remarked above, however badly the Portuguese ruled the people went their own way in domestic and commercial life and did an immense amount of good to the country by introducing new products, such as the cashew *(kishu)* nut and tobacco. They also vastly improved the spices and fruits for which Malabar was already famous. Especially was their work beneficial to the cultivation of the cocoanut; and they may be said to have created the great modern trade in coir. So, although there is much to be said against the Portuguese doings in South India, it cannot be truthfully asserted that they produced no good at all.

R. C. Temple.

Montreux
Switzerland.

CONTENTS

INTRODUCTION

For the study of Portuguese relations with Malabar there is available in India, England and in Portugal, a very large mass of material. It consists mainly of large collections of State papers, official despatches and other correspondence, descriptive narratives, besides records of a more personal character like the "Commentaries" of Albuquerque and the biography of de Castro. Neither is there any lack of "histories," for the Portuguese writers of those days were not forgetful of the duty of singing the glory of their fatherland. In India also, there is a considerable quantity of highly valuable material, mostly in the form of Chronicles in the Malabar temples and royal families.

A thorough examination of the documents and papers relating to India, preserved in the various libraries and archives of Portugal, was made by Mr. Danvers of the India Office Library. He also secured for the India Office translations and transcripts of the most important of these. As a result, the India Office Library now possesses a unique collection of Portuguese manuscripts. Their value would have indeed been greater if the translation had been undertaken by someone who had a better knowledge of English than the Portuguese scribe to whom the task was entrusted. As it stands, it is often difficult to make sense out of whole passages, and often it is easier to consult the original than to go to the translation. The following are the chief collections and unpublished books available at the India Office.

I. The Corpo Chronologico. Transcripts 2 vols. These are translated. They consist mostly of letters addressed by Governors and other officials to the King and sometimes to important court dignitaries in Lisbon. This collection is of the utmost importance.

II. Gavetas Antigas. Translations 2 vols.

III. Translations as well as transcripts from the Cathedral library at Evora and the letters from Viceroys which are preserved in the Torre de Tombo.

IV. Noticias da India. 2 vols.

This is a very interesting, though often undependable, collection of descriptions of forts and places of historical interest.

V. Biker's collection of Treaties and Engagements with Indian Rulers. Two volumes are translated.

VI. The Cartas of Albuquerque. 4 volumes are translated.

At the Torre de Tombo and the National Library of Lisbon there are many valuable documents not yet available in England. Through the courtesy of Dr. Antonio Baio I was enabled to examine a good many. Unfortunately, though the material relating to India is vast, Malabar finds but little mention after the time of Albuquerque. The "Documentos remittidos da India," which is a monumental series of 62 volumes covering no less than 12,465 documents, hardly touch Malabar. It covers the period between 1600 and 1697. For our purpose the most important collection is the Corpo Chronologico. It is on this I have had mainly to depend.

In the British Museum there is an excellent collection of Portuguese MSS. besides a number of interesting portraits.

The Portuguese Academy has been for considerable time actively assisting in the publication of important documents and books relating to India. The most important publication of the Academy in this connection is the Colleccao de Monumentos ineditos para a historia das conquistas dos Portuguezes em Africa Asia e America. The Annæs das sciencias e letteras have also published some very important documents which were until then unknown.

Portuguese histories relating to India are numerous. The most important of them are the following:

(1) Joas de Barroes, whose official connection with the India Office in Lisbon gives his work, which is practically a contemporaneous record, an authority which few others possess.

(2) Gaspar Correa. Lendas da India. This book also is of special importance. Correa went to India in 1512. He acted as Albuquerque's secretary and the events he describes were therefore known to him personally or related to him by those who had taken part in them. With regard to the first voyage of Vasco da Gama he had the benefit of using a diary which Joam Figuera,

who accompanied the Captain-General in that expedition, had kept. His *Lendas*, it is curious to note, remained unknown till 1790, and was published only in 1886.

"I laboured," says he, "with much care on the events I saw and those which had gone before enquiring of the older men who had been of this discovery and removing my doubts by means of the same men who had been present at the events: in the course of which I found some men who had come in the very ships of discovery. Also by means of some memoirs which I found in the possession of Moors and Gentiles, especially in Cannanore who wrote with surprise at seeing what they had never imagined."

The Chapters relating to the voyages of Vasco da Gama in this book have been translated by the Hon. H. E. Stanley for the Hakluyt Society (1869).

Other histories like the works of Diogo de Couto and Castenheda, valuable though they are, do not devote much space to Malabar affairs.

Besides these volumes which are of primary importance, I have used the following books:

I. Andrade, J. F. Life of Dom John de Castro. translated into English by Sir Peter Wyche, 1664.

II. Barbosa, Duarte. Hakluyt Society, 1866.

III. Caldwell. Comparative Grammar of Dravidian Languages. 2nd edition, 1875.

IV. D'Albuquerque. Commentaries translated and published by the Hakluyt Society.

V. Danvers. Portuguese in India. W. H. Allen, 1894, 2 volumes.

VI. Da Orta. Colloquies—Lisbon. 1895. Edited by the Conde de Ficalho. English translation by Sir C. Markham, London, MCM XIII.

VII. Ficalho, the Conde de. Garcia da Orta e sua Tempo Impresna Nacional.

VIII. Logan. Malabar. 2 volumes. Madras, 1887.

IX. Menon. History of Kerala. Ernakulam, Cochin Government Press, 1925.

X. Pages, Leon. Lettres de St. Francois Xavier. Paris, 1885.

XI. Rawlinson. The Relation of India with Western Nations.

XII. Sousa Faria y. Portuguese Asia. translated into English 1695.

XIII. Whiteaway. Rise of the Portuguese Power in India. comes up only to 1545.

XIV. Zeinuddin. Tofut ul Mujahideen.

XV. Fra Coleridge. Life and Letters of Francis Xavier. translated by Rowlandson; Murray, MDCCCXXXIII.

XVI. Gouvea. Historie Orientale des grand progres de Chretianisme. Anvers, 1609.

Apart from these I have also had ample opportunity of using unpublished original material available in Malayalam. There is in Malabar an ancient custom of keeping *grantha varies* or chronicles in the chief temples and royal families. These have so far remained unpublished. Owing to the kind help rendered to me by Rama Varma Appan Tampuran of Cochin I have been able to procure copies of these documents from which I have occasionally drawn for the details of Malabar history. There is also available, in Malayalam, an historical account of Portuguese relations with the Malabar princes, written probably in the 17th century.

It now remains for me only to express my many obligations. To Sir Richard Temple, (Bart.) C. B., C. I. E., F. B. A., I am deeply indebted for the valuable foreword which he has written to the book; to His Highness Rama Varma Appan Tampuran of Cochin, a generous patron of all arts, for his kindness in securing me the copies of temple chronicles; to Andre Furtado of Lisbon, whose scholarship in Portuguese and excellent knowledge of English were of considerable help to me in Lisbon; and to Prof. Edgar Prestage, Member of the Portuguese Academy and Professor of Portuguese at King's College, London, for advice and help in many matters connected with Portuguese manuscripts. To all these gentlemen I express my sincere and heartfelt thanks.

K. M. Panikkar.

MALABAR AND THE PORTUGUESE

CHAPTER I

MALABAR BEFORE THE ARRIVAL OF THE PORTUGUESE

Malabar extends from Mount Delli N. Lat. 12° 2′ to Cape Comorin. It forms a single geographical and ethnical unit, preserving in many ways a singularity of customs and social organisation which mark it off as a separate entity in India. Cut off by the Western Ghats from intercourse with the people on the eastern coast, Malabar has, from the earliest times, been in direct contact with the sea-faring peoples of the West. The main maritime trade routes in ancient times, as in the present day, lay through the Arabian coast and the Red Sea, and through them the trade of Malabar flowed into Europe. The wide prevalence, on the Malabar coast, of curious customs like ear-lobing, shank worship and other elements of heliolithic culture, always found in combination, has been proved by Professor Elliot Smith to have been the result of early Phoenician connection.[1] We have ample evidence of other kinds also to prove the close contact of Malabar with the Euphrates valley and the Mediterranean countries. Logs of Indian teak have been found in the temple of the Moon at Mugheir and in the Palace of Nebuchade-

1) See Elliot Smith—"Migration of Culture"—Ryland Library Memoirs 1918.

nezzar.[1] It has been held on philological evidence that the Hebrews, at the time of Solomon, knew of Malabar. Bishop Caldwell states that the word for "peacock" in the Hebrew text of the Books of Kings and Chronicles in the list of articles of merchandise brought from Ophir (circa 1000 B.C.) in Solomon's ships is the Tamil word *tokai* which in Hebrew became *tuki.*[2] Cinnamon and Cassia, which are produced mainly in Malabar and Ceylon and are foreign to Palestine, were much in use among the Hebrews.[3]

This trade continued to flourish, and was mainly in the hands of Egyptians and Asiatic Greeks. With the growth of the imperial power of Rome, the trade with Malabar increased in volume. Both the Greek and Roman geographers such as Eratosthenes left descriptions of voyages to the West Coast of India. Though these works have perished, much of the information contained in them is incorporated in the works of Strabo (1st century B. C.), of Diodorus and of Pliny. Strabo, himself an Asiatic Greek, noticed at the Port of Myos Hermos much trade with Indian ports, and mentions that 120 merchantmen sailed for India in a single season. Myos Hermos was the centre of trade with Malabar, and Pliny the elder has left an account of a voyage from that port to the Indian coast. "To those bound for India," says he, "it is most convenient to depart from

---

1) The whole evidence is discussed in Rawlinson's—"The Relation of India with the Western Nations".

2) Caldwell—"Comparative Grammar of Dravidian Languages", 1875 2nd edition, London p. 91-92.

3) Exodus XXXV, 23, 24.

Okalis (in the Red Sea). They then sail with the wind Hippalos in 40 days to the first Emporium of India, Muziris. There reigned when I write this Kalabathros."

The whole course of trade with India underwent great change when in 45 A.D. Hippalos made the epoch-making discovery of the Monsoon winds. He observed that these winds in the direction of India were seasonal, and conceived the idea of utilising them for commercial voyages. From that time it may be said that Western trade with Malabar ports has been continuous and unbroken. As this discovery synchronized with the great development of Roman power in the East, there grew up between the Malabar ports and the Roman Empire a flourishing trade of no mean volume and importance. Embassies from South India visited Augustus, Claudius and Julianus. Roman merchants regularly visited Malabar ports, and the trade in spices grew to such importance that when Alaric spared Rome in A.D. 408, he demanded and obtained as a part of the ransom three thousand pounds of pepper, then as now, the main product of Malabar. Sewell states that the Puertinger tables mention a temple of Augustus at Cranganore with a small Roman settlement; but this is very doubtful as neither the edition of Kanad Muller nor the Leipsic facsimile mentions Muziris.

The discovery of large quantities of Roman coins, of all ages from Augustus, proves that this commerce with Rome continued to flourish unbroken for a long time. In the collection of The Maharajah of Travancore there are 9 aurei of the reign of Augustus, 28 of Tiberius, 2 of Caligula, 16 of Claudius and 16 of Nero.[1] Roman money was practically in current use, as hoards of coins have been found all over Malabar from Pudukkadu, near Cannanore, to Kottayam in Travancore.

The main port in Malabar which was the centre of this trade, as Pliny says, was Muziris or Cranganore. It was known in Malabar as Muyirikkodu—it is so mentioned in the so-called Christian plates. The earlier Tamil poets allude to it as Muchiri. Periplus mentions that "Muziris is a city at the height of prosperity frequented as it is by ships from Arriake and by Greek ships from Egypt." The exports of Malabar consisted mainly of "Pearl, in considerable quantity and of supeiror quality; pepper in larger quantities and gems of every variety." The imports were mainly coral, lead, tin, stibium, etc. It will be noticed that the trade which the Romans carried on with Malabar was practically in the same commodities as those in which the Portuguese traded at a later time.

It is as a result of this close connection with Arabia, Egypt and the West that Malabar came to have in its midst a community of Jews and St. Thomas Christians. Of the exact time of the arrival of the Jews and the Christians, we have no definite information. We have evidence that they were flourishing in Malabar in the 7th Century. Besides these communities, there was a powerful trade guild of Chetties, which carried on commerce with Arabia and Egypt as well as with

1) "Roman Coins Found in India"—Sewell—J. R. A. S. 1906—Jouveu Dubreil: Indian Antiquary—March 1923.

the Far East, called Manigramam which, on no evidence at all, has been claimed to have consisted of Christians. The only reason for such assumption is that when Gen. Macaulay discovered the plates awarding rights to Manigramam, he thought they belonged to the Christians and handed them over to the Syrian Church. The Tanu Ravi plate specially mentions that it was granted to Eravi Korttan, the head of the Manigramam. That the Manigramam was a Hindu trading guild can be seen from the fact that the temple and the tank of Sri Narayana in Takopa in Siam is, according to an inscription found there, placed under the protection of the Manigramam.[1] The inscriptions of Tiruvellerai, near Trichinopoly, point to the same fact. What is of importance to us here is that the Manigramam was a powerful trading association whose activities extended all over Malabar.

In mediæval times Malabar trade had passed into the hands of Mahommedan merchants. The importance of Malabar increased, as it was in the direct line between Arabia and China. The Arab traveller, Solyman, mentions that Chinese ships touch Quilon on their way to the Persian Gulf, which port, according to him, was the most considerable centre of trade in Southern India. A Sanskrit poem of the 9th Century mentions that its commerce is such that it is the cynosure of all the eyes of the world.[2] Marco Polo

1) J. R. A. S. 1913 pp. 337-339.

2) Suka Sandesam "Lōka thrayyāmakhila thanubhrillōchaneikāvalambē Kōlambēsmin".

noticed later that merchants from China and from Arabia and from the Levant came thither with their ships and their merchandise and made great profits by what they imported and by what they exported.[1] From him we get an idea as to what were the main commodities available in Malabar at that time.

"A great deal of Brazil is got here which is called Brazil Koilumin from the country which produces it. It is of very fine quality. Pepper too grows in great abundance. They have also abundance of very fine indigo."[2]

Ma Huan, the Chinese traveller, mentions that Quilon was known to the Chinese navigators of the 7th Century. But the supposed Chinese colony to which historians have alluded, following Yule, is a mistake arising out of a wrong interpretation of Misar bin Huhalhil's statement that "when the King of Quilon dies the people of the place choose another from CHIRVA", which Yule interpreted as China. Chirva or Chirava is a small place not far from Quilon where a collateral branch of the family resided, from among whom it was customary to adopt into the royal family. Ancient Malabar records constantly mention adoptions between the families of Chirava and Quilon.[3]

The Western trade of Malabar from the beginning of the 8th century passed into the hands of the Muslims. The growth of an Arab empire, extending from Sind to Morocco, gave an impetus to Malabar trade and helped Malabar ports to establish close connection

1) Marco Polo—Vol. II, p. 375.

2) Malabar—Vol. II, pp. 284-285.

3) See Sloka, 117—"Unni Nili Sandesam" B. V. Book depot, Trivandrum, 1922.

with Cairo, Tunis, Bussorah and other Mahommedan ports, which continued up to the time of Vasco da Gama's arrival. The Caliphs of Baghdad were enthusiastic supporters of maritime enterprise, and, under Caliph Omar, the town of Bussorah was founded as an emporium of trade with India. The stories of Sinbad the Sailor bear witness to the adventurous spirit of the Arabs in pursuit of commerce; and this extraordinary activity was felt in an increased demand for Malabar products in the West.

The rise of Venice as the great maritime power of the Mediterranean brought India into further intimate contact with Europe. The policy of Venice was to keep the trade of the East with Europe in her own hands; and by alliances and treaties with Mahommedan Powers like the Sultan of Egypt who commanded the sea route, she was able, for a considerable time, to maintain a monopoly over it. The prosperity of Venice, resulting from her trade with India, was a matter of extreme jealousy to other European Powers; and one of the chief motives that led the Genoese and the Iberian nations to enterprises of maritime exploration, leading to Vasco da Gama's discovery, was the desire to get direct to India without the intervention of Venice or Egypt.

The political and social conditions of Malabar at the end of the 15th Century immediately before the arrival of the Portuguese on the scene presented some striking features. The whole area from Cannanore to Cape Comorin was divided into a number of petty principalities over each of which ruled a Raja or some less pretentious chief who vaguely acknowledged the suzerainty of one of the major rulers. Both Indian and foreign authorities agree that at the close of the 15th Century only the Kolathiri or the King of Cannanore, the Zamorin or the King of Calicut and the Tiruvadi —as the Portuguese authorities call him—the King of Venad had what we may call full sovereign rights.[1] Apart from these rulers, there were the minor Rajahs of whom the chief were the Rajahs of Tanur, Cranganore, Cochin, Mangat, Idappalli, Vadakkumkur, Procaud, Kayamkulam and Quilon. The effective power in the land was in the hands of the Kaimals and Kartavus, independent nobles who maintained armies of their own, and owed allegiance sometimes to more than one sovereign. The major rulers, like the Zamorin, often claimed and exacted many rights over these lords; but as the strength of the great rulers was dependent on the willing subordination of the smaller Chiefs, the policy pursued by the suzerains was to leave them to themselves as far as possible. Malabar Law did not recognise the right of the sovereign either to depose a rebellious Chief or to confiscate his property. The Tofut ul Mujahideen mentions, with regard to the Zamorin, that "whenever he commenced hostilities with any of the considerable Chiefs of Malabar after subduing them, it was his practice to return to them their possessions, and the restitution, although sometimes delayed for a long time, he made always in the end."[2] The chief lords of this kind were the Iruvanad

1) Duarte Barbosa, page 150.
2) Tofut ul Mujahideen, page 59.

Nambiars and Cheranchery Kurup in Cannanore territory; Kavalappara Nair, Koratty Kaimal, Mannarghat Nair, Punnathur Nambidi and others in the Zamorin's territory; and the Anchi Kaimals who held Ernakulam and the coastal tracts in Cochin. It should be remembered that the allegiance they owed was mainly for military support in time of war. The suzerain could not interfere in their internal affairs, nor stop them from going to war against each other. In fact, there was, strictly speaking, nothing in the nature of royal power in Malabar. The difference between the political organisation in Malabar and the feudal system which it resembles superficially lies in this fundamental fact. In many ways, the Nair lords resembled feudal barons, especially in that they had to provide soldiers when their suzerain went to war with another ruler. But the feudal principle was entirely absent from Malabar, because the Lords were themselves the owners of the land and did not hold it even nominally of the King. There is in fact every reason to believe that the political organisation of Malabar developed from small local communities, each holding independently of the other.

Though the lords and minor Rajahs of Malabar had the rights of private war, of entering into alliances and treaties with others and of levying customs, yet social opinion did not permit any but the Kings of Cannanore (Kolathiri), Calicut and Travancore to wear crowns, to coin money or to hold ceremonial umbrellas over their heads. These were considered the insignia of royalty. At the time the Portuguese reached

India, the Rajah of Cochin had none of these dignities[1]. The Rajah of Cochin claimed superior social status, he being a Kshatria while the Zamorin belonged to the Nair caste. This was felt as an indignity and much of the history of the Portuguese in Malabar can be understood only in the light of this fact.

Of the position of Calicut at the time of the arrival of the Portuguese we have ample records, both Indian and foreign. The Indian records, literary and historical, are unanimous that it was a great city and a flourishing port, one of the most important in India, which carried on trade with all parts of the world. Abdur Rezzak, the Ambassador of Shah Rokh, noted in 1443 that Calicut was so flourishing a port "that merchants from every city and every country came together there. In it are to be found abundance of precious articles brought thither from maritime countries... Security and justice are so firmly established in the city that the most wealthy merchants bring thither from maritime countries considerable cargoes which they unload and unhesitatingly send into the markets and bazaars without thinking in the meantime of any necessity of keeping watch over their goods."

Nicolo Conti described it as 'a noble emporium for the whole of India'. Ludovic de Varthema writing between 1503-1508 describes the country of Calicut at great length and confirms the view of the earlier writers of the great prosperity of the town and the general security of its government.

1) Duarte Barbosa, p. 107—"Kerala Charitam", 113.

Calicut was a town about 8 miles in circumference. The population consisted mostly of Hindus, but there was a considerable number of Mahommedans from Ormuz, Cairo, Abyssinia and even Tunis. They had built two mosques in the city where they met for their Friday prayers. The whole foreign trade of Calicut was practically in their hands. The Arab traders never interfered in the politics of the state and for this reason were held in high esteem by the rulers of Calicut. Besides, through them the state of Calicut was able to equip its army with better arms and secure Arab horses; and much of the power of Calicut as against the other states rested on this.

The Zamorin Rajahs who ruled Calicut from the earliest days belong to the Nair caste. Though originally their supremacy in Malabar was questioned by the Valluvanad Rajah who had the support of the Pallavas of Kanchi, by about the 13th Century the Zamorin became the leading ruler on the west coast. His effective sway extended from Cannanore to Quilon. The area south of Quilon was held by the King of Travancore who never acknowledged the sovereignty of the Zamorin. The Kolathiri Rajah of Cannanore was also practically independent; but the area between the Kingdoms of Cannanore and Travancore obeyed the command of the ruler of Calicut.

The government of Calicut was an autocracy tempered on the one hand by the power of the semi-independent vassal Chiefs who were perpetually in revolt, and on the other, by the sacerdotal power of the

Major; "India in the 15th Century" pp. 14-15.

Nambudiri Brahmins, who, like the Catholic Church in the middle ages, constituted a supra-national body owning but very shadowy allegiance to the temporal power. The great Nair Chiefs, who were independent in their territory, consisted of some of the hereditary officials of the state and others who were merely vassal rulers. These often fought among themselves and sometimes combined to defy the authority of their suzerain.

The administration of Calicut was carried on under the direct orders of the Zamorin and his ministers. Duarte Barbosa notes that the King of Calicut "keeps many clerks in his palace. They are all in one room, separate and far from the King, sitting on benches and there they write all the affairs of the King's revenue and his alms and the pay which is given to all and the complaints which are presented to the King, and at the same time the accounts of the collection of taxes. There are seven or eight who always stand before the King with pens. These clerks always have several leaves subscribed by the King in blank and when he commands them to despatch any business, they write it on these leaves."[1] The city of Calicut had a separate Governor and a customs officer.

The Kingdom of Kolathiri which lay to the north of Calicut had, as its principal city, the port of Cannanore. This port also carried on great commerce with Mecca and Surat.[2] The country that lay inside was fertile and produced much fruit, aromatics and spices. The Kolathiri Rajahs never recognised the suzerainty of the

1) Duarte Barbosa, 110.
2) "Noticias da India"—Vol. I, p. 221 seqq.

Zamorin and were always at war with him. Their Kings considered themselves Kshatrias and therefore higher in social status. The Kolathunad country also was divided up between Nair Chiefs who maintained armies, fought against each other and intrigued with the Zamorin.

The other important Kingdom was Travancore. This state extended from the city of Quilon down to Cape Comorin. Tofut ul Mujahideen states that the King "who possessed the greatest number of soldiers was Tiruvadi, Rajah of Quilon and Kumaree,[1] whose country lay between and to the east of those towns and whose territories were of considerable extent." Ansteley's Collection of voyages also allude to the Rajah of Travancore as a powerful and independent ruler. Its original history is shrouded in mystery, but from about 1250 we have authentic record by which to trace the growth of its power. In that year the family of Quilon was left with only a princess who married a prince of the Chirava family named Jayasimha who thereupon assumed royal power. From him the territory took the name of Jayasimha Nad—or Singanatti as the Portuguese call it. His son Ravi Varma is an important figure in the history of South India. He conquered the Pandya and Chola Kingdoms and had himself crowned at Kanchivaram where he had his victories inscribed on stone. He fought against Malik Kafur who invaded South India under the orders of Allauddin Khilji and when the Mahommedan army withdrew,

1) Zeinuddin, p, 58 59.

he was able to strengthen his authority all over South India. He reigned at Quilon at the beginning of the 14th Century. Many branches of this family, each reigning over small tracts are mentioned in Malayalam books. Of these the most important are Trippappur and Attungal. In the latter place only women had the right to rule, the males being considered, according to seniority, as head or members of one of the other branches. This custom is still preserved in the Travancore family, the Senior Maharani of Travancore being always the Princess of Attungal and enjoying the hereditary possessions of that principality.

Of the minor princely families, the most important was that of Cochin. This family belongs to the Kshatria caste and claims descent from the last Perumal or Emperor of Malabar. But, whatever might have been their claims for independence in earlier times, these had entirely disappeared by the end of the 13th Century. The Zamorin, as has been pointed out, was lord and master; and, even in the domains immediately surrounding Cochin, authority was shared between the Rajah and the different Nair barons. The Cochin Rajahs had the curious custom, found among other important families of Malabar also, of forcing the eldest person into retirement on the pretext of desiring religious meditation. As a result of this, there were always two parties, one taking orders from the abdicated ruler and the other from the reigning sovereign, a position which almost invited the interference of the powerful King of Calicut.

North of Cochin on the backwaters was the principality of Cranganore, whose rulers were subject to the authority of the Zamorin. The *Noticias da India* mentions that the territory of Mangat lies to the east of Cranganore. Further up the river, adjoining Mangat, was the principality of Parur the ruler of which was a Nambudiri Brahmin. In the terrtiory of the Zamorin which lay to the north of these the Nair barons had less power. He kept them in check, though the Chief of Kavalappara, near the present station of Shoranur, and the Rajahs of Nilambur enjoyed great power.[1]

To the east of Cochin on the other side of the backwater lay the land of Idappalli, also ruled by a Brahmin Chief. The rulers of Idappalli were the friends of the Zamorin and served him as an advance guard against the Rajah of Cochin. It was in Idappalli that the great battles, in which Duarte Pecheco won his fame, were fought. Idappalli provided for the Zamorin the base for operations against Cochin, and the campaigns, in the period we have to describe in the chapters to follow, always opened by an invasion into the very heart of Cochin from the side of Idappalli.

South of the territories of the Rajah of Idappalli lay the important territory of Vadakkumkur. Its capital was the town of Kaduthirithi, a few miles to the south-east of Vaikom. The Portuguese allude to Vadakkumkur as "the pepper country", as the finest pepper produced further inland had to come to them through this state. The Rajahs of this place are Nairs

1) "Noticias da India", Page 226.

by caste and are alluded to in ancient documents as "Vadakkumkur Nair." Though nominally subordinate to the Rajah of Cochin to whom they were allied by marriage, the Vadakkumkur Rajahs enjoyed full ruling authority and had very considerable military strength, as the Portuguese found out on more than one occasion. Another branch of the same family ruled further south.

The marshy land consisting of the present Taluq of Ambalapuzha and the eastern portion of Changanacherry was under the rule of a Brahmin Rajah who bore the hereditary name of Deva Narayanan. This Chief had a considerable naval force under him which was commanded by a family of Arayars. Between Procaud and Quilon lay the state of Kayamkulam or Kallikoilon. Though the Chief of this state was not very powerful, his state enjoyed considerable importance from the commercial point of view, as Kayamkulam was the natural outlet for the fertile country which lay to the interior. Politically, the area behind was split up even more than the territories of Cochin or Calicut. In the small district of Tiruvalla alone there were 10 Brahmin families who ruled with equal authority.

The absence of royal authority, which was thus the main characteristic of Malabar polity, had early in the 15th Century begun to undergo a slow change. The establishment of the great Hindu Empire of Vijayanagar whose authority extended to the borders of Cannanore had its influence on the political conditions of Malabar. Besides, Calicut had become by this time the great centre of Western trade and the Zamorin was easily the wealthiest and the most powerful ruler on the coast. He had assumed the style and dignity of a great King and begun to call himself the Lord of the Hills and the Sea. His naval forces were strong enough to scour the coast from Gujerat to Ceylon. Even more than this, the Zamorin had the support of the Moorish settlers who contributed so largely to the prosperity and power of his kingdom. With their help he was extending his power in such a way that in the century immediately preceding the arrival of the Portuguese he had practically become the King of all Malabar from Cannanore to Procaud and exercised royal power in a way that no other Malabar ruler had done.

Besides the local traditions, what stood in the way of the Zamorin setting himself up as an autocratic monarch in the style of the Kings of Vijayanagar or the other rulers of the east coast was the curious religious polity of Malabar. Politically divided into small principalities, Malabar was one from the point of view of social and religious organisation. The very fact that there were no Kingdoms and states but only Rajahs and Chiefs, who had often rights and properties in each others' territory helped the growth of an extra-political social unity. In the temples of Cochin and even of Travancore the Zamorin had many rights. In the territories directly under the sway of the Zamorin there were many temples in which minor Chiefs who did not owe allegiance to him exercised authority. The Rajah of Kayamkulam had special rights in the temple of Kutalmanikyam in Iringalakuda in the territory of the

Cochin Rajah, which have now passed over to the Travancore Government. Besides this, the position of the Nambudiri Brahmins was also definitely ex-territorial. Like the Catholic Church before the Reformation, the Nambudiri Brahmins did not recognise political boundaries; and what is more, the Rajahs, themselves, had no such territorial notions as to expect powerful religious or social organisations within their areas to yield unitary obedience to them. Most of the temples with their enormous revenues were in the hands of the Brahmins. Even the Sri Padmanabha pagoda at Trivandrum, which is one of the most ancient foundations in Malabar and one of the richest, is governed by a body of eight members, and the Maharajah, whose family temple it is, has only half a vote.

With the power of the territorial magnates so well established, and the authority of the religious organisations placed clearly above political divisions, it was impossible to develop in Malabar a central government with all-embracing authority, except by a process of slow evolution. The expansion of the Zamorin's power, based on the support of the Moors, had begun to do this with some success and his authority had slowly penetrated down to the borders of Procaud when the Portuguese arrived on the scene.

Some account of the main divisions of population in Malabar and their relation to each other is necessary for a clear understanding of the history of the Portuguese connection. The population of Malabar is divided vertically into Hindus, Christians, Mussulmans and Jews, and horizontally into Nambudiris, Nairs,

Tiyas and other castes among the Hindus, Moplas and Arabs among Mussulmans, and White and Black Jews among the followers of Judaism. Among the Hindus, the Nambudiris, though numerically small, stood out as a theocratic oligarchy which managed its own communal affairs without any considerable intervention of temporal power. They were also large landholders, and, by the peculiar system of primogeniture which confined inheritance to the eldest member of the family, who alone married in his own caste, they preserved their property intact and maintained their social influence. Though mainly devoted to Brahminical pursuits, the Nambudiris had, among them, a few ruling families who held small tracts of land and exercised political power like Nair Chieftains. Such were the Rajahs of Parur, Procaud and Idappalli. The whole district of Tiruvalla, to the north-east of Kayamkulam, was divided between ten Brahmin families. Between the Nambudiris and the Nairs there was from the beginning the closest connection, as the younger members of the Nambudiri families, who could not marry in their own caste, formed matrimonial alliances with Nair women.

To understand the position of Nairs in Malabar society and their internal organisation at the time of the arrival of the Portuguese, we have ample material in European languages. All the earlier Portuguese writers devote considerable space to a description of Nair character and customs. We have also the descriptions left to us by the early travellers, such as Marco Polo, Ibn Batuta and Abdur Rezzak.

The Nairs were more a community than a caste. We have even now evidence of a former priestly class among them whose authority and importance diminished as a result of the superior position of the Brahmins. But apart from priestly functions, the Nair community consisted of three main divisions: the Samantas or the ruling castes, to which the leading royal families such as that of the Rajahs of Calicut, Vadakkumkur, Mangat and the vast majority of minor Chiefs belonged; the large classes which constituted the militia of Malabar, and the lower classes such as barbers, washermen, potters and weavers. Though all these were equally Nairs, the term Nair is generally confined by Western writers to the first two classes. They form the predominant community on the coast. Their authority was restricted only by the sacerdotal claims of the Brahmins.

The two chief characteristics of the Nairs were the matriarchal system of family life[1] and their military organisation. Even to this day, the Nairs are matrilineal in descent and are organised in family groups known as Tharawads, in which the relationships are counted exclusively on the mother's side. Each family thus constituted a fairly large unit, with a membership often going up to over a hundred. Each of these families was under the *potestas* of a Karanavan, who was the eldest male member on the mother's side, and he enjoyed the same rights as a *pater* in a Roman *familias*. Thus each family was practically organised as a unit

1) *Vide* "Nair Family Life." Journal of the Royal Anthropological Institute. London 1919.

for military service, because social obligations pertained not to the individual but to the family.

To the warlike character of the Nairs, the Portuguese as well as other foreign records of the time bear ample witness. They were organised into Janjadams or groups, and each member of the group was bound by oath to avenge the death of other members. Every Nair of the first two classes was trained in a Kalari or a Gymnasium for a number of years where the use of all arms was taught by specially trained teachers. In every village, there was an Āsān or instructor in warfare to whom special honour was paid. The youths of the families of the village were compelled to undergo military instruction and follow the Āsān in time of war. Every Nair was attached to some Kalari, and the Kalaris themselves were attached to some ruler. There was thus a system of practical conscription among the Nairs. The Rajahs and Chieftains depended for their authority on the Nair militia who thus enjoyed almost a monopoly of political influence in the country.

The other Hindu communities like the Tiyas were agricultural labourers. They were not permitted to share in the civic and political life of Malabar and were much oppressed by the Nairs.

The Christians of Malabar formed an important community with special privileges and rights of their own. In origin, they are said to have come from Syria, Baghdad and the Persian Gulf. From the time of Jacob Albardi they owed their spiritual allegiance to the Eutychian Patriarch, and, taking after the name of Jacob Albardi were known as Jacobites. The great majority of them, as their own tradition declares, were converts from high caste Hindus, Nambudiris and Nairs, though at a later period a considerable number of lower caste men seem also to have been converted. They followed all professions, commercial and agricultural, and were also recruited into separate companies for warfare by some Chieftains. Unlike the Nairs who were spread over the whole of Malabar the Christians lived in groups in various places. Their most important centres were Cranganore, Kunnamkulam, Udaimperoor in Cochin territory, and along the valley of the Pampa river and at Quilon.

Socially, the Christians occupied an important position. Important communal privileges and absolute religious freedom had been guaranteed to them from the earliest days of their existence in Malabar. They were governed by their own *Metrans* or Bishops, some of whom were sent out from the seat of the Archiepiscopate at Bussorah. Politically also they enjoyed considerable influence. There is a tradition that they had amongst them a ruler of their own known as the Rajah of Villiarvattam. The tradition of an extinct royal family of that name is still prevalent in Malabar; but accounts vary as to whether it was Brahmin or Christian in religious faith. However that be, before the Portuguese arrived on the scene, the family had become extinct.

The Jews lived mostly in Cranganore, which was the place they had originally settled in. They were divided into Black and White Jews, the former being of mixed descent. They migrated to Cochin only during the struggle between the Portuguese and the Zamorin when life in Cranganore became unsafe owing to constant depredations by the rival powers.

The most important non-Hindu people, who were next only to the Nairs in political power and influence, were the Moors. They consisted of Arab settlers and Moplas of mixed descent. It is reasonable to suppose that as at least after the time of Caliph Omar the trade with Malabar was exclusively in the hands of the Moors, the Arab community in Malabar dates from the early 8th Century. There were powerful Moorish settlements all over the coast, the most important being at Calicut which was the centre of Moorish trade. The naval forces of the Zamorin were under their command, and it was with their military help that the Zamorin succeeded in vanquishing his rivals. They had a complete monopoly of seaborne trade and their commercial relations extended as far west as Tripoli and Morocco. Ibn Batuta declares that the Moors of Malabar were extremely rich, that one of their leading merchants "could purchase the whole freightage of such vessels as put in there and fit out others like them." The Mammalis and Khoja Musas whom the Portuguese encountered were merchant princes to whom Cairo and Damascus were as familiar as Calicut and Cannanore. Through them, the Zamorin was in close connection with the rulers of Egypt, Persia and the Northern Indian Sultanates.

Though they wielded so much influence with the Malabar rulers, it is true, as Zeinuddin has pointed out, that the Mahommedans of Malabar refrained from encroaching on the rights of the people. "I would have it understood," says he, "that the Mahommedans of Malabar[1] lived in great comfort and tranquillity in consequence of their abstaining from exercising any oppression towards the people of the country as well as from the consideration which they invariably evinced for the ancient usages of Malabar and from the unrestricted intercourse which they preserved with them." The friendly feeling between the Nairs and the Moors was based on mutual tolerance and a recognition that in social matters each community should be allowed to live its own life. "Notwithstanding that the rulers and their troops were all pagans, they paid much regard to their prejudices and customs and avoided any act of aggression on the Mahommedans except on extraordinary provocation, this amicable footing being the more remarkable from the circumstances of the Mahommedans not being a tenth part of the population."

As a result of this, the political power as well as material prosperity of the Moors gave rise neither to jealousy nor to fear; and everywhere on the coast the Moors were encouraged by the Malabar Rajahs to establish centres of trade.

Thus, at the end of the 15th century, Malabar was leading a comparatively happy, though politically isolated, life. In many ways, her oraganisation was primitive; but she had evolved a system in which trade flourished, different communities lived together without

1) "Tofut ul. Mujahideen" page 103.

2) Ibid. page 71.

friction, and absolute religious toleration existed. The wars of the Chieftains did not materially affect the tranquillity of her life, and in town and country alike law and order were enforced. The weakness of the system was that though there were many Kings and Rajahs there was no such thing as royal authority, no central power capable of uniting the Nairs into a single confederacy. Undoubtedly, the course of Malabar history during the two centuries previous to the arrival of the Portuguese was in the direction of an increase of the Zamorin's power and the establishment of a Malabar confederation under his authority. But this very process gave rise to jealousies and feuds. It is this fact that should be clearly borne in mind in the study of Portuguese influence in Malabar.

CHAPTER II

VASCO DA GAMA'S VOYAGE

In the navigating activities of the 15th century, which were mainly conceived with the object of circumventing the Mahommedan control of the Red Sea Route to India, Portugal played an important part. The desire for maritime exploration and discovery was given a great and lasting impetus in that country by the adventurous spirit and career of Dom Henry, Duke of Viscau, better known to the world as Prince Henry the Navigator. It was Prince Henry who conceived the idea of reaching India by rounding the southern point of Africa. In his expeditions Prince Henry was loyally supported by his father and later on by his brother. Besides this royal encouragement, he had at his command the immense resources of the Order of Christ of which he was the Grand Master. That the wealth of this religious Order should be used for the purpose of exploration was nothing strange, because Prince Henry, like a devout Christian, regarded his discoveries as the conquest of new worlds for Christ. It is important to remember this because the policy of the Portuguese in the East becomes intelligible only in the light of the firm belief which they entertained, till the very end of their supremacy in the Indian Seas, that their work was the work of God and, therefore, as against them, no body of men, unless they be Christians, had any rights.

Prince Henry's discoveries encouraged him in the project of claiming for Portugal the right of sovereignty over all the new lands in Africa and Asia. In 1441 he made a request to the Pope to grant to the Crown of of Portugal such territories as may be discovered beyond Cape Bojador. Dom Henry did not fail to point out that as a Christian prince he considered it his first duty that the heathen peoples of the lands discovered should be claimed for Christ. The *Curia* agreed to grant his request, and a Papal Bull was issued giving the crown of Portugal the exclusive rights of sovereignty in Africa and Asia.

Information about the seas on the other side of Africa was by this time slowly trickling down to Europe. The Venetians had presented to Dom Pedro, the brother of Prince Henry, a copy of Marco Polo's Travels with a map of the world as the Venetian traveller knew it. In a map made for King Affonso in 1460, the eastern coast of Africa was traced and marked by Fra Mauro, a Venetian friar. Dom João II was as enthusiastic as his predecessors and even more determined. His first attempt in this direction was to select João Peres de Covilhão, a fidalgo who knew Arabic well, for a journey to India by land. Accompanied by Affonso de Paiva, Covilhão started from Lisbon in the first week of May 1487. Leaving Paiva at Aden, he took a boat to Malabar reaching Cannanore by the traditional route of Greek and Roman trade. He stayed for a considerable time both at Cannanore and at Calicut and gathered valuable information about Indian trade. On his return journey, Covilhão, however, was forced to stay in Abyssinia where he died after many years of service.

The maritime expeditions that João II organised were even more successful. Two ships of 50 tons each were fitted out in 1486 and their command was entrusted to Bartholomeo Diaz. Diaz rounded the Cape of Good Hope and thus the way was opened for an expedition to India. João II recognised the importance of the discovery in opening up the passage to India, and it is in recognition of this fact that he gave to the promontory the name of the Cape of Good Hope. Dom João thereupon took up with enthusiasm the organisation of a more ambitious expedition which was to reach India direct. He began the preparations immediately. He had already received valuable information about the route to India from the King of Benin during the latter's visit to Portugal in 1484. Before his project could materialise, Dom João died (1496). Dom Manuel who succeeded him, though of a less idealistic nature, inherited in full the enthusiasm of his family for maritime discovery and took up the project with zeal. In this he had the advice of the Hebrew Astronomer Abraham Ben Zakut. In consultation with him, the necessary preparations were made. Three ships were specially constructed with a view to stand a prolonged voyage on the high seas and all due care was taken to provide for contingencies and unforeseen circumstances. The ships were built on the plans of Bartholomeo Diaz, and their construction took over a year. The accumulated experience of over half a century of exploration and voyage, and the information systematically gathered from various sources from the time of Dom Pedro were utilised[1] fully in the methodical preparation of the great undertaking. The armada was ready in 1497 and the King, to the surprise of all, entrusted its command to an unknown courtier, a fidalgo of his Household, Vasco da Gama.

Vasco da Gama was the third son of Estevão da Gama and his wife Isabel Sodré. On both sides he was descended from noble stock. The da Gamas were a well-known family tracing their descent to a knight who accompanied Quialdo the Fearless. Another da Gama was a famous general in the time of Affonso III, and yet another, Alvaro da Gama, fought with Affonso IV in the battle of Salado.[2] The Sodrés, of whom we shall hear a great deal in connection with India, were an equally well-known family.

The family seat of the da Gamas was in the town of Sines where the church built by Vasco can still be seen. Here it was that the future navigator was born in 1469. Vasco became a Gentleman of the Household of the King, Dom Manuel. It was when he was in that position that he was selected to command the expedition. The reason for this selection is obscure. There was nothing in the previous life of Vasco as a courtier to entitle him to the command of an armada. The reason that Barroes gives is that the original idea was that of Estevão da Gama, the father of Vasco, and Dom

1) Reade J. R. A. S. 1898 P. 589.

2) Estevão himself was the Controller of the Household of King Affonso.

Manuel nominated Vasco as a recognition of his dead father's claims.

The ships were fully equipped, provisioned, and were ready to set sail. The voyage was blessed by ecclesiastical dignitaries. The voyagers were absolved of all sins by virtue of a Bull which Prince Henry the Navigator had obtained for the benefit of those who may die without the comforts of religion in the middle of the sea. On July 8th the whole crew heard Mass and then from Belem the armada sailed. On which ship Vasco da Gama himself was is not definitely known. Correa, who wrote his history with the help of the diary of a priest who accompanied the Captain-Major, states that the flag-ship was San Rafael, while Barroes who is more reliable as a historian, states that San Gabriel was the ship on which Vasco himself sailed. The generally accepted view is that San Gabriel was the flag-ship. According to modern conceptions these were hardly more than small sailing vessels. San Gabriel was not more than 120 tons while San Rafael was even of less capacity. But they were heavily armed for their size—San Gabriel carried no less than 20 guns. The rigging consisted of 3 masts with six sails. It is on a ship like this that the voyage to India was undertaken.

Rounding the Cape after a stormy voyage, the armada reached Mozambique in March 1498. There Vasco da Gama captured an Indian named Davane. After many adventures, the ships reached Melinde at the end of April. There the Portuguese captain was received with honour. After an exchange of presents, ceremonial visits, etc., the King who was well disposed towards the Portuguese offered da Gama Arab pilots who knew the seas well and could direct him to Calicut. Between the African Coast and Calicut there was a regular trade in spices; and it was at the King of Melinde's suggestion that the decision was taken to sail to Calicut instead of to Cambay. With the help of the Melindian pilot the Arabian Sea was crossed without difficulty in 20 days' time. The land first sighted was near Cannanore, but the Portuguese did not anchor there. Sailing down the coast, they anchored off Kappat, a few miles to the north of Calicut on May 17th.[1]

The discovery of the sea-route to India was a great event from the point of view of the results that followed from it. But as a feat of exploration, or even of nautical adventure, it was of no importance.

The historical results that have flowed from the direct contact of European Powers with India and the commerce and wealth which the control of the Indian seas has given to Europe, have shed an exaggerated light on Vasco's achievement. It should be remembered that the project of a voyage to India round the Cape did in no sense originate with Vasco da Gama. He had in fact nothing to do with the conception or the planning of the project. It had already been planned by Dom João following the traditional policy of Dom Henry; and in this Dom João had at his disposal the expert advice of Abraham Ben Zakut. Even the

---

1) It is characteristic of Portuguese historians that they are not agreed even as to the month in which Vasco da Gama reached India.

instructions to Gama were drawn up in consultation with him. The discovery of the Cape of Good Hope by Diaz had partially fulfilled the dream of Dom João; and the plan itself was matured and its organisation undertaken by Dom Manuel, on the basis of authentic information gathered by the court during half a century of exploration. Moreover, India was in no sense a *terra incognita.* It was in close contact with Europe, through the Venetians and the Moors. Besides, the sea-faring people on the Coast of Africa, consisting mainly of Arabian settlers, knew the routes and the winds, and da Gama had the help of competent Arab pilots supplied to him by the King of Melinde. He was not sailing in uncharted seas like Columbus or Magellan, but sailing along recognised routes to a country which was situated at a known distance from the African coast. There is nothing in Vasco da Gama's discovery which entitles him to the claim of a great explorer or navigator. His glory is based entirely on the historical results that followed, for which he was hardly responsible.

The real importance of the new "discovery" lay in the fact that it broke the monopoly which the Venetians and the Egyptians had so long enjoyed in the trade with India. Before that time no European nation since Alexander's time had come into direct contact with India. Egypt, by its natural position, had stood as the intermediary between India and the West. The arrival of da Gama with his two ships at Calicut was the end of India's political isolation from Europe. Till then her intercourse with outside peoples was confined to those that lived on her north-west frontier. Indian rulers had not realised the possibilities of sea power and the political strength that it can bring. Vasco da Gama created for India a new frontier and with it new political and commercial problems.

The effect of this was not immediately recognised in India. Indian Powers, accustomed to look only to dangers from land forces, did not realise the menace to their security implied in the two ships which had reached the Malabar shore. The only people who realised the far-reaching significance of this event were the Moors who saw that their trade supremacy was endangered and fought desperately against the newcomers. Both the Egyptians and the Turks saw the true extent of the danger and were prepared to meet it. But internal complications, resulting mainly from the conquest of Egypt by the Turks, gave the Portuguese a short respite during which they were able to consolidate their naval position, from which, even if they did not advance, they were never fully dislodged till the Dutch entered the field.

CHAPTER III
VASCO DA GAMA

Da Gama arrived at Kappat or Capucad, a few miles north of Calicut. A large number of people gathered on the shore to see the vessels which were of a kind different from those usually navigating the coast. It was decided by the Portuguese, after a consultation, not to go on shore without hostages. Da Gama also circulated the story through some fishermen that his ships were merely the advance guard of a numerous armada with which he had parted company. Communications were opened with the Zamorin's officers who were extremely friendly. The Zamorin's pilots took the ships inside the harbour at Pandarini Kollam where they were safe from storms. The Portuguese captain and his friends were invited to land. Da Gama, with a number of his officers, landed on shore and travelled inland to where the Zamorin was at the time. A curious incident happened on the way. Seeing a Hindu temple where the priest was conducting a religious ceremony, da Gama and his companions, mistaking it for a Christian Church, went in and worshipped.

The Zamorin received the party in a special durbar. Da Gama was careful to let it be known widely that he represented a very powerful King. Besides, as Correa himself says, there were many Moors at the Calicut court who were well acquainted with the conditions and politics of Europe and who must have informed the ruler as to who these foreigners were and where they came from. Gama presented himself at court dressed "in a long cloak, coming down to his feet, of tawny coloured satin, lined with smooth brocade and underneath a short tunic of blue satin and white buskins and on his head a cap with lappets of blue velvet with a white feather fastened with a splendid medal; and a valuable enamel collar on his shoulders and a rich sash with a handsome dagger."[1] He was accompanied by a page dressed in red satin, and in front of him went the men in single file.[2] The King watched their arrival from a balcony. Gama was received at the gate of the palace by the commander of the bodyguard, without whose permit no one could enter the palace. The King received them "seated on a rich bed set out with silk and gold in a room arranged with silk stuffs of various colours and of white canopy which was of subtle workmanship and covered the whole room."[3] The Zamorin was clothed "in white cotton strewed with branches and roses of beaten gold[4] but wore many ornaments of great value." Correa says, "He had on his left arm above the elbow a bracelet which seemed like three rings together, the middle one larger than the others, all studded with rich jewels particularly the middle one which bore large stones which could not fail to be of very great

1) Correa—"Three voyages," page 192.
2) Correa—"Three voyages," page 193.
3) Faria y Sousa, page 47.
4) Faria y Sousa, page 47.

value; from this middle ring hung a pendant stone which glittered; it was a diamond of the thickness of a thumb. Round his neck was a string of pearls about the size of hazel-nuts, the string took two turns and reached to his middle. Above it, he wore a thin round gold chain which bore a jewel of the shape of the heart,[1] surrounded with larger hearts and all full of rubies; in the middle was a green stone of the size of a large bean, which, from its showiness, was of great price, which was called an emerald." The Zamorin was attended by his chief officers. Behind him stood a page boy armed with a drawn sword, "a red shield with a border of gold and jewels, and a boss in the centre, of a span's breadth, of the same materials, and the rings inside for the arm were of gold."

After the presents were placed before the King, da Gama was ushered in. Compliments were exchanged and the Captain-Major made a speech explaining his mission and the desire of the Portuguese King to open commercial relations with India. He also presented to the King kneeling, the letter of Dom Manuel. The letter was received with great courtesy, but beyond that the negotiations did not proceed. The Zamorin's answer to the request for commercial facilities was vague, and da Gama was asked to communicate to the Treasurer of the King what commodities he wanted. The parting was cordial, and the Portuguese and the people of the town met in friendly intercourse. But da Gama was not satisfied. The kind of stuff he had

---

1) Evidently a *pathakkam* which is an insignia of royalty in Malabar.

brought from Lisbon for exchange in India was not suited to the Indian market and there was no demand for them from the Indian side. The Portuguese attributed this to the intrigues of the Moors and complained to the Zamorin that the goods were not being sold. Whatever the cause was, there was but little trade done between the Portuguese and the local inhabitants.

Soon, the Zamorin, who was residing a few miles out of Calicut, sent for da Gama in order to have another interview with him. The Portuguese, always suspicious that others were intriguing against them, were particularly nervous, and in this feeling they were confirmed by certain words which a Castilian resident at Calicut dropped in a low tone to da Gama when he was starting on the journey. Portuguese historians, with that genius for seeing in every incident a miracle and every skirmish a battle, have regaled their countrymen with stories of treachery and patient endurance in the face of misfortune. Nothing in fact had happened to justify the fears the Portuguese entertained. The Zamorin had merely asked for the goods to be unloaded. In fact, for the inconvenience that da Gama had suffered in coming so far into the interior, the Zamorin expressed his regret.

When the monsoon season was over da Gama made preparations for returning to Portugal. He requested the Zamorin for permission to leave a factor at Calicut in charge of the merchandise which he was not able to sell. The Zamorin required customs to be paid according to the regulations of the port; but this da

Gama refused to do. It was this controversy that embittered the relations of da Gama with the Zamorin and helped to convince the latter that the new-comers were bent not merely on commercial pursuits. Da Gama sailed away from Calicut as soon as the Monsoon season was over, taking with him a few low caste captives whom he had held as hostages.

Leaving Calicut on the 29th August 1498, da Gama sailed north and reached the port of Cannanore. At the invitation of the Kolathiri Rajah who had a hereditary feud with the Zamorin who was always attacking his country and threatening his independence, Gama landed there. The Rajah of Cannanore was naturally anxious to be on friendly terms with the Portuguese and offered them all facilities for trade. The Zamorin had already warned the other rulers of Malabar about the Portuguese, but this did not deter the Kolathiri from entering into an informal agreement with them and helping them to load their ships. From Cannanore they set sail on the 20th of November. The ships put in at Anjediva, a group of small islets on the Malabar coast, where some time was spent in repairing and refitting the vessels. Here Gama also came across a Jew from Grenada who had become a Mahommedan, and carried him to Lisbon. This Mahommedan was converted to Christianity under the name of Gaspar da India.

Da Gama reached Lisbon on the 29th of August. The successful return of the armada caused great rejoicings in Portugal. The fleet had been absent for over two years. The whole court gathered at the port of Belem near where the great cathedral of St. Jeronymus now raises its stately head. The nobility, the clergy, the ladies of the court, all mingled to get a sight of the "hero" who had made the greatest sea-voyage of the age and discovered the sea-route to India. The King, Dom Manuel, was himself awaiting him attended by the Household. As the ship drew near and anchored at the harbour, Jorge de Vasconcelos, a chief noble of the Household, was sent by the King to convey the greetings to the Admiral. When Vasco got down from the ship, his appearance was indeed striking. His majestic figure was made more striking by the flowing beard which had never been shaved or trimmed since leaving Portugal. Dressed in a close-fitting silk jacket, but with no ornaments, he walked straight up to where the King was. Dom Manuel stood up to receive him. After a long audience, during which da Gama described his adventures in detail, he drove with the King to the palace where he was presented to the Queen. Honours and titles were showered upon him. The title of "Dom" along with the perpetual right of 200 Cruzados a year was given to him.

From the commercial point of view, da Gama's voyage was a great success. The cargo he brought with him was worth 60 times the cost of the expedition and the King was naturally anxious that the resources which were thus opened out to him should be exploited in full. A new expedition was fitted up with Pedro Alvarez Cabral as commander. The

* "Three Voyages," page 230.

instructions given were to persuade the Zamorin to drive out the Moors, and if unsuccessful in that to proceed to Cannanore. His armada consisted of 33 ships and carried 1500 men. Among those who were associated with Cabral were Bartholomeo Diaz and Nicolas Coelho. After a very eventful voyage, in which chance led him to the coast of Brazil, which was thus "discovered and taken possession of" by the Portuguese, Cabral reached India with only 6 ships.

The Portuguese King could not have selected a worse officer if he wanted to establish peaceful relations with the Indian rulers and carry on trade. Cabral had neither tact nor foresight. He had an overweening pride which suspected an insult in every innocent movement, and was short tempered. On arriving at Calicut, he sent on shore, dressed in Portuguese costume, a low caste fisherman whom Gama had taken to Europe, with a message to the sovereign. In a country like Malabar which is caste-ridden this was the greatest possible insult. Though the Zamorin would not see the messenger, an interview with Cabral was arranged. On September 18th the Zamorin met Cabral, but the interview broke up owing to a misunderstanding. Cabral, thinking that his person was in danger, returned in a hurry to the ship, leaving the cargo and the Portuguese who accompanied him on the shore. Negotiations were then resumed between the Zamorin's plenipotentiaries and Aires Correa, as the agent of Cabral. After prolonged discussions extending over 2½ months a settlement was reached which gave the Portuguese the right of having a factory in Calicut.

The Portuguese in the meantime began to claim extraordinary rights on the sea. Their idea is thus put by Barroes:

"It is true that there does exist a common right to all to navigate the seas and in Europe we acknowledge the rights which others hold against us; but this right does not extend beyond Europe; and therefore the Portuguese as Lords of the Sea are justified in confiscating the goods of all those who navigate the seas without their permission."[1]

Under cover of this convenient theory Cabral seized a ship belonging to the Arabs that was at anchor at the harbour. His complaint was that the Arab ships were able to load pepper which he wanted for himself. The Portuguese were already putting forward claims of monopoly; but the native traders sold naturally to those who paid them the best price. Cabral complained of this to the Zamorin who replied that they were welcome to buy as much as they could pay for. But Arab competition was keen; and dissatisfied with the method of having to bid and buy in the open market, Cabral hit upon the easy way of attacking and taking possession of Arab vessels within his reach. Up to this, the Nairs on the coast had been friendly with the Portuguese. They had treated them with courtesy and done business with them. In fact, the Portuguese themselves recognised the friendliness of the inhabitants and had only few weapons with them in their camp on shore. But the news of Cabral's

1) Barroes, Vol. I. Bk I.

unwarranted aggression caused anger and consternation, as the people of Calicut had, for many centuries, been accustomed to complete security of property and person. The populace was roused to fury, and in the riot that ensued the factory was destroyed and more than half the Portuguese on land were wounded.[1]

Cabral retaliated in his brutal fashion. He massacred the crew of all the boats he could lay hands on in the harbour, in some cases burning the ships with the men in them. The coast area of Calicut is occupied mostly by low caste fishermen with thatched huts and consequently the action of the Portuguese did not cause much material damage, though the effect of the bombardment on the people in general must have been to strike terror. It confirmed in the minds of the Nairs of Calicut the belief that the intruders were uncivilised barbarians, treacherous and untrustworthy. It made the Zamorin an enemy and Calicut the most determined opponent of Portuguese connection as Affonso Albuquerque found out later on.[2]

Cabral soon discovered that further stay in Calicut was useless and might possibly become dangerous. The coast was unknown to him and the monsoon was about to set in. At the suggestion of the converted Jew, Gaspar da India, it was decided to sail to Cochin. He reached that port on Christmas Eve 1500. There was with Cabral in his boat a Malayali Christian, named Michael Jougue, belonging to the Syrian church, who had embarked with a view to go to Palestine. Cabral

1) "Kerala Charitam", p. 21.

2) Cartas, p. 130.

sent him along with a Portuguese to seek an interview with the Rajah of the place. The residence of this prince was at Kalpathi, on the northern river, overlooking the sea. There the envoys of Cabral interviewed the Rajah[1] who was naturally pleased to hear about the quarrel between the new-comers and the Zamorin. Permission was immediately granted to the Portuguese to buy whatever they wanted, and Cabral, disappointed at Calicut, found in Cochin a docile ally whose submission to his plans was likely to be of great importance to Portuguese power in the East.

Cabral himself visited the Rajah and presented him with a variety of things which he had especially brought from Portugal. An informal treaty was arranged by which permission was granted to the Portuguese to build a factory in Cochin. As the experience of popular fury in Calicut had taught him to be cautious, Cabral requested that some leading Nairs might be sent to the ship as hostages, and this was agreed to. As a result of the whole-hearted support given by the ruler, the ships were loaded without difficulty in a very short time. At the same time, messengers arrived from Cannanore and Quilon inviting the Portuguese to these towns and promising them satisfactory trade arrangements.

The effusiveness with which the Cochin Rajah welcomed Cabral, and the ease with which negotiations were concluded, were due to the humiliation which the Rajah felt in being a subordinate of the Zamorin. Cochin was at that time a very small principality

1) Correa—" Lendas da India "—Tomo I—Chapter IX.

dependent on Calicut. It was the privilege of the Zamorin to settle even the succession to the Musnad. The Cochin Rajah had no right of coinage, and the Zamorin even interfered in matters of administration. The chief noblemen in the state, especially the Anchi Kaimals who held the territory on the coast, were the supporters of the Zamorin and defied the Cochin Rajah's authority with his help. It was a humiliating position for the Rajah, and, for some considerable time past, he was intriguing to throw off this galling yoke. In the Portuguese adventurers, an exaggerated version of whose exploits he had heard through Michael Jougue as well as through the Mahommedan merchants, he thought he had found allies with whose help he would be able to free himself from the control of the Zamorin. But, Unni Rama Varmah who made the alliance little foresaw the misfortunes and humiliations which awaited this change of allegiance. The Portuguese Governor became in a short time his lord and master, and made the Cochin Rajah drink to the very dregs the cup of humiliation in exchange for the ready help he had given him.

In the meantime the Zamorin did not remain idle. In the short period of a fortnight, he equipped a fleet of about 80 ships carrying about 1500 men. When they were sighted off Cochin, Cabral's courage deserted him. At night, he fled taking along with him even the Nair hostages who were on the ship.[1] One of them, a relation of the Rajah, was treated with special

1) He abandoned even those Portuguese who were on land numbering about 30, including Duarte Barbosa the writer.

honour by Cabral and was presented to Dom Manuel who took a great liking for him. He was made a noble of the court and given vast estates in the country. He was carefully educated in Portuguese, and later on converted to Christianity when he took the name of Manuel. He was employed to draft the King's letters to Malabar Princes. He lies buried in the cathedral at Evora where his tomb can still be seen.

Sailing hurriedly, Cabral anchored at Cannanore, in the country of the Rajah of Chirakkal who helped him to load some further cargo. Thence, he left for Portugal.

The first naval encounter with the Indians did not end in favour of the Portuguese. But this was due to the incapacity of the commander. We have sufficient evidence to show that the people of Malabar were as good seamen as the Portuguese. But events were soon to prove that on sea, as on land, equipment is the deciding factor. The equipment of the Portuguese ships was the very best of the time, excluding perhaps the ships of the Turkish navy. The fire-arms which the Portuguese used were a novelty in India; and it is these facts that settled the fate of India's command of the sea. But, in spite of all this, for a very long time, in fact till 1599 when the fort of the Kunjalis was taken, Indian ships continued to harass Portuguese trade and cause them great damage.

Besides the five ships, which were all that were left of the armada of thirteen, laden with the spices and the merchandise of the East, Cabral took with him a letter from the Rajah of Cochin to the King of Portugal, and many valuable presents for the Queen. The royal letter was written on gold leaf, and professed friendship to the royal family of Portugal and expressed the Rajah's pleasure at the trade relations which were established. The presents for the Queen included ornaments studded with precious stones and a large quantity of the best silk.

The alliance with Cochin was important in two ways. The Rajah of Cochin, being a discontented and powerless prince, was a willing tool of Portuguese ambition. He saw in the new power of the foreigners an easy way of gaining his independence. The Zamorin's interference with his affairs, which mainly took the form of deposing the ruler at the time of the accession of the Zamorin and installing a new one, and of compelling all Cochin products to be sold through the port of Calicut, had the result of creating a smouldering discontent in the hearts of Cochin Rajahs. They were therefore glad that an opportunity had come by which they could profit.

Secondly, the Cochin harbour, unlike the port of Calicut provided a base which could be defended from the sea. What the Portuguese wanted was not a trading factory, but a port in which they could establish themselves. The factory in Calicut, as it was on the mainland and surrounded by the Zamorin's men, could not be defended against hostile attack. Cochin is on a small island, separated from the mainland by the backwaters and so narrow that every part of it could be shelled from the sea. Its acquisition gave the Portuguese a strong foothold from which no land Power could expel them. Besides, Cochin was in the centre of Malabar, a suitable point for controlling the politics and trade of the country. Behind it lay what the new-comers called "the great pepper country," and the backwaters provided an excellent line of communications. Moreover, from a political point of view, Cochin was especially suited for the exercise of their power. Around the town were a number of small Chieftains, all fighting against each other. The *Noticias da India* mentions the Chief of Mangat, a few miles to the east of Cochin, and the Chief of Parur, a few miles to the north, as rulers of importance; while it states that the country surrounding Cochin was in the hands of Kaimals. To the south-east lay the small but important principality of Vadakkumkur. Two miles to the east of Cochin was the Brahmin principality of Idappalli, and to the south the peninsula of Shertallay was divided up between 73 petty lords. There was no prince powerful enough to resist Portuguese aggression and the result was that, with Cochin as their centre, they were able to intimidate and domineer over the neighbouring areas.

The long absence of Cabral caused the Portuguese King to send out a small fleet of 4 ships under João de Nova. On the way he was able to get full information as to what happened to Cabral at Calicut and Cochin. Taking warning from the disasters of both da Gama and Cabral at Calicut, de Nova avoided it and sailed to Anjediva where he was met by the emissaries of the King of Cannanore. Before going to Canna-

1) p. 225—p. 230.

nore he decided to find out what happened to his compatriots at Cochin. Nova found that at Cochin the merchants refused to exchange goods and insisted on cash. As he was not plentifully supplied with gold, he left for Cannanore in the hope that he might be able to realise money by selling European goods at that port. But the Mahommedan merchants had organised a successful boycott. Finally, through the help of the Rajah who stood guarantee, he was able to load his ships, and return to Europe.

The return of Cabral dissipated the earlier optimism about India. It was now recognised that even the sovereignty of the seas which the Portuguese King had claimed for himself as "the Lord of the navigation, conquest and commerce of Ethiopia, Arabia, Persia and India," would be keenly contested. But Dom Manuel was prepared for any sacrifice and fitted up a new armada to be sent to the Indian waters for the purpose of retaliating against the Zamorin and of effectively asserting the authority of the Portuguese in the Arabian Sea. Cabral was first nominated as admiral. But the King showed a lack of confidence in him, and da Gama himself volunteered to go.

The new armada consisted of 15 ships. The captains who accompanied da Gama whom Barroes mentions by name were Luis Coutinho, Francesco de Cunha, João Lopes Perestillo, Affonso d'Aguiar, Ruy de Castenhada, Diago Fernandez Correa who was nominated as captain of the factory of Cochin, and Antonio de Campo. The flag-ship San Jeronymo, in honour of the patron saint, was under the command of Vincent Sodré, a relative of da Gama. Of the 15 sails six were large vessels including San Jeronymo and Lionarda commanded by Coutinho, and five were lateen-rigged caravels fitted with heavy artillery. Altogether, they carried 800 men in arms. The soldiers who had joined the expedition were to be paid 8 cruzados a month besides two quintals of pepper for every 18 months they spent outside Portugal.

On the 30th of January 1502, the King heard Mass at the cathedral of San Jeronymo, and in a speech made da Gama admiral of the Indian, Persian and Arabian Seas. The fleet sailed from Belem on the 10th of February. The King himself went out on his barge. Out of the fifteen, ten under the admiral were to return after taking effective measures to secure the whole commerce of the Indies for Portugal and after punishing the Zamorin against whose power all these preparations were made. The other five under Vincent Sodré were to form a permanent Eastern squadron stationed in the Indian seas. A month and a half later another squadron of 5 vessels under Estavo da Gama left for India. This armada is probably the biggest that went out to India before the 19th Century. It was equipped and sent out with a view to conquest, because the Portuguese King had finally realised that a monopoly of the trade of India cannot be obtained except by an effective control of the sea.

On the way, the Portuguese fleet committed numerous acts of piracy. A ship belonging to a brother of Khoja Kassim of Calicut was returning from Mecca. Da Gama stopped it and plundered the goods. "The

Captain-Major", says the admiring author of *Lendas da India,* "after making the ships empty of goods, prohibited any one from taking out of it any Moor, and then ordered them to set fire to it." No pleading could assuage the thirst of the Portuguese for blood; and though the Moors offered all they possessed, the order was given to set fire. This is a typical example of the inhuman and almost demoniacal cruelty of the Portuguese adventurers, and we shall meet with many more as the story progresses. What is astonishing is that the Portuguese historians have no word of disapproval for this horrible and cruel massacre, and even Camoens passes the incident without mention.

Da Gama reached Anjediva which was made the base of operations. In order to fulfil the first part of the orders to him, which was to establish a monopoly of trading in the Indian seas, the ships separated and began capturing all merchant vessels seen on the high seas. They gathered a rich harvest. On reaching Cannanore, the King of Chirakkal came with 4,000 Nair swordsmen to see him. An interview took place on a scaffolding on the sea side.[1] The Rajah was given various presents including a sword of gold and enamel. A commercial treaty was discussed but it was not possible to settle the prices as the merchants said that the King had only the right to the duties. Finally, it was agreed that they should receive the same prices in Cannanore as in Cochin. Vincent Sodré was left behind in Cannanore with instructions "to buy and

1) Correa says it took place in a house.

gather in the warehouse rice, sugar, honey, butter, oil, cocoanuts and dried fish, and to make cables of coir."[1]

From Cannanore, da Gama sailed to Calicut. He found the harbour cleared. According to Barroes, the Zamorin sent four messages to the Captain-Major, the final one being when da Gama was only two leagues from Calicut. In these messages, he pointed out that if any one had a complaint it was he. He was however prepared to make an agreement. Gama insisted as a preliminary of peace that all Mahommedans in the city should be expelled, and as the Zamorin refused to consider so impossible a demand, Gama immediately began a bombardment of the city. The Zamorin had huge barricades erected with palm trees, but considerable damage was done by the fire. The Nairs of the shore also attempted to reply with the help of two guns. The rice vessels that arrived during these days were plundered and their crew captured. The Captain-Major ordered his men "to cut off the hands, the ears, the noses of all the crews and put them all into one of the small vessels in which he ordered them to put the friar (a Brahmin envoy of the Zamorin who came with a Portuguese safe-conduct) also without ears nor nose nor hands, which he ordered to be strung round his neck with a palm leaf for the King on which he told him to have a curry made to eat of what the friar brought him."[2] The vessel was then set on fire. The Zamorin, on hearing of this outrage for which it is

1) "Three voyages," page 325.
2) "Three voyages," vol. I, page 331.

impossible to find a parallel in history, swore "to expend his whole kingdom" to fight the Portuguese.

After a futile bombardment for 3 days, da Gama sailed to Cochin. He reached that port on November 7. There the Portuguese, whom Cabral in his haste had left behind, met him and described to him how the Cochin Rajah had saved them from the enmity of the Moors and even allowed them to sleep in his own palace. The Rajah also sent envoys to greet him. The next day, the Captain-Major went on shore and presented the Rajah with various gifts which he had brought from Portugal in return for the letter and presents that the Rajah had sent. These included 2,000 gold Cruzados enclosed in a large silver cup. The Rajah was well pleased and allowed the Portuguese to load their ships with merchandise. After a few days, during which five large vessels and two small ones were laden with pepper, cardamom and other spices, da Gama appeared in his true colours. He presented his terms of alliance to the Rajah which were, first that all pepper, cardamom and other spices must be sold to the Portuguese at a price to be fixed between the Captain-Major and the Rajah, and secondly that the Portuguese should be given the right of building factories and keeping garrisons in places where they wished and that no one else should be allowed to do so. The Rajah was taken aback. He had welcomed the Portuguese as friends, but now he found that they had come as masters. In his chagrin, Unni Rama Varmah asked for time to consider the demands. Gama rose in anger and left the conference demanding that an answer should be given then and there. The poor Rajah followed him and begged his forgiveness. He promised to agree to whatever terms the Portuguese desired. That was what da Gama wanted. On the acceptance of the terms, the Rajah was given many valuable presents including a gold crown.

In the meantime, the Zamorin made great preparations. He collected a large naval force under Koja Kassim with a view to attack da Gama off Cochin. Da Gama's anxiety was to escape with his booty to Europe; so leaving Diogo Fernandez Correa as the factor in Cochin he sailed off to Portugal. When he was about to leave, the Rajah of Cochin made an appeal to him explaining the precariousness of his position, how the Zamorin was organising a great expedition against him, and how members of his own family, the nobles of his state and even a part of his army had declared for the Zamorin as against the Portuguese. The issue was stated clearly by the King of Calicut. In his final letter before the outbreak of the war, the Zamorin asked the Rajah of Cochin as to whether he wanted the friendship of the foreigner or the friendship of Calicut.[1] To all this appeal by the Rajah of Cochin da Gama turned a deaf ear. He had his ships laden. His interest now was to return with them to Lisbon. He escaped from Cochin, like a thief at night, on the 9th of December leaving the Cochin Rajah to his fate.

One thing of special interest which happened while da Gama was at Cochin was the interview which took

1) "Kerala Pazhama", page 35.

place between him and representatives of the local Christians. These men, believing that with the arrival of the Christian Portuguese the time of good fortune and greatness had come for them, approached him and offered their allegiance to the King of Portugal. They suggested that if a fort was built by the Portuguese in the area where they were strong, the whole of Malabar could be conquered. They little knew what persecutions, miseries and outrages they were to suffer at the hands of these Christian Portuguese, whom they thus invited to conquer Malabar.

CHAPTER IV

THE FIGHT FOR LAND POWER

The welcome which the Cochin Rajah gave to the Portuguese and the treaty that Cabral made with him brought upon that unfortunate prince the wrath of his overlord. The secret clause of Cabral's treaty was that the Portuguese would help to make the Cochin Rajah independent of the Zamorin and instal him as the chief ruler of Malabar. Twelve years later, when the great Albuquerque succeeded in making peace with the Zamorin by abandoning this ambition of placing a puppet King of the Portuguese as the sovereign of Kerala, the King of Cochin, Unni Rama Varmah, who signed the treaty with Cabral, wrote to the King of Portugal in the following words:

> "After all this had taken place they came to me at this my port and I assisted them with all they asked me for, both in cargoes for their ships and all the other things... It has from that time appeared to all my friends and enemies that the friendship existing between Your Highness and myself could not be severed on any account and this they knew for certain that Your Highness sent me a golden crown as a sign that I was crowned the chief-king and your chiefest friend."[1]

The Zamorin recognised the danger which lay in the alliance between his vassal and the Portuguese. It

1) Bikers Treaties, Vol. I.—Torre de Tombo C. C. P. 1 Maco 14.

was clear that if the Portuguese were allowed to establish themselves in Cochin, the independence of the Malabar Princes was not safe. The Zamorin knew enough about the cruelty and treachery of the newcomers. He asked for their surrender, or, in case the Cochin Rajah's honour forbid that, their expulsion from Cochin. The Rajah, proud of his new alliance, and believing in the promise of the Portuguese to make him the ruler of Malabar, refused to yield, though the Zamorin's request was supported by his own officers, nobles and leading generals.

On refusal, the Zamorin moved south with his army. He had as his main allies the Rajah of Idappalli, whose state was but two miles away from the town of Cochin, and the Patingettedam Nambudirippad a Brahmin nobleman who held the environs of Trichur. With their help, the Zamorin marched into the heart of Cochin without any resistance. At this time, Vincent Sodré with his squadron arrived at Cochin; but, in spite of the earnest requests of the Portuguese in the fort and of the Rajah, he refused to help in the defence and sailed away on the excuse that it was the best time of the year to plunder Mahommedan ships in the Red Sea. There he met with a tragic fate, his squadron and most of the men being destroyed in a terrible gale that overtook him near the Curia Muria Islands. On March 1, 1503, the war between Calicut and Cochin began. In the early skirmishes, success lay with the Cochin Rajah. This was mainly due to the efforts of Lorenco Moreno with whose help the Cochin forces defended the fort at Idappalli with great courage.

But the Zamorin, attacking both from the sea and from the land, carried the position and the Cochin forces withdrew a little inside. In the battle that took place there the Cochin army was annihilated, and three Cochin Princes, including the heir apparent who was the commander-in-chief, were killed. The Cochin Rajah gathered another army and attempted to stem the tide of invasion and failing to do so, took sanctuary, along with his Portuguese allies, in a temple.

The Zamorin again sent envoys to the Rajah of Cochin. He declared that he only wanted that the Portuguese should be expelled. This request was again refused. The Zamorin carried fire and sword into the enemy's territory, and, after establishing a strong garrison at Cochin, returned to Calicut.

The monsoon interfered with the course of the campaign and the Zamorin stayed at his capital for the next three months. But the time was not wasted. The Ruler of Calicut recognised that if the foreigners were to be successfully resisted it could only be done with their own superior weapons. For this purpose, he employed in his service two Italians, Pero Antonio and Joa Maria, who undertook to cast cannon for him and to teach his soldiers the use of it. From that time, warfare with the Zamorin took a new turn; and during the whole period that the Portuguese played their part in India, they were never able to subdue him, though by stratagem and by policy they gained some temporary advantages.

By the end of the monsoon time, three small squadrons from Portugal arrived in Indian waters. The first to reach was the squadron under Francesco d'Albuquerque who was followed by his cousin Affonso Albuquerque (later on Governor) with three ships, while a similar force under Antonio de Saldhana arrived a few weeks afterwards. Francesco Albuquerque heard of the whole course of events in Cochin while in Cannanore and sailed immediately southwards with a view to bring help to Cochin. Francesco drove out the Zamorin's garrison from Cochin and built there, on the pretext of helping the Rajah, the first Portuguese fortress. The Rajah supplied the necessary material and the foundations for the fort were laid on the 27th of September 1503. The structure was in the form of a square of 183 yards surrounded by a deep moat. The Rajah himself came and encouraged the builders, little knowing that he was loading the pistol against his own breast. The fort was named after Dom Manuel. The Rajah of Cochin was indemnified by a gift of 10,000 Cruzados and the Portuguese captain extolled the great generosity and wonderful loyalty with which the Rajah had defended the Portuguese refugees in the days of their greatest trial.

The Zamorin's forces had retired from the immediate neighbourhood and the allies lost no time in taking revenge. One incident in this otherwise uninteresting compaign deserves mention as illustrating the methods of the Portuguese in carrying on war. Near Cochin there was a Chieftain by the name of Cheruvaippil Kaimal who was lord of 3,000 Nairs. The Portuguese captain, with the help of the Rajah, surrounded his castle and, after defeating his troops, set fire to the town killing men, women and children. The Rajah of Idappalli was especially the object of their inhuman revenge. They burnt his villages, desecrated the temples, carried off women and children into slavery. They mercilessly laid waste whole tracts through which they passed and ravaged the population like a plague.

After the retirement of the Zamorin to his own territory, the Portuguese pointed out to the Rajah the necessity of dealing with his own Chiefs. The first agreement of importance that he made with his own barons was the treaty with the Anchi Kaimals, the powerful lords who held the territory on the mainland side of the Cochin river. By this treaty, which may be said to lay the foundation of the Cochin Rajah's effective sovereignty in his own state, the Kaimals accepting definitely the Rajah's suzerainty over them, swore allegiance to him and his family, and agreed to hold their estates of him. This treaty is of great importance, because it is the first testimony of the course, which the Portuguese attempted to follow as a part of their policy, that of aggrandising their power with the small Chieftains under cover of a nominal suzerainty of the Cochin Rajah.

A truce with the Zamorin was arranged but the Portuguese did not keep it for long. They attacked some of the boats carrying pepper and other merchandise belonging to the subjects of Calicut and war was again declared. Information regarding the preparations the Zamorin was making was brought to Albuquerque by a Mahommedan spy. The Portuguese captain was anxious to stay and fight the Zamorin's forces, but his soldiers were bent on reaching home. Leaving Duarte Pacheco with about 90 effective men to defend the fortress of Cochin, the work on which was by this time completely finished, and after provisioning it to stand a siege, the Albuquerques left for Lisbon. Frencesco and his ship never reached Portugal.

The Zamorin prepared his attack with great care. He knew that on account of the ravages of the Portuguese, no cultivation had taken place in the area around Cochin, and that rice, the staple food of the people, was scarce. In the circumstances rice had to be imported from the Carnatic coast. The Zamorin persuaded the Mahommedan merchants to desist from this, and Ismail Marakkar, the head of the Mahommedan community, issued orders prohibiting the trade in rice with Cochin. But Duarte Pacheco was an able and resourceful man. He had the leading Muslim merchant of Cochin and his family kidnapped and held as hostages for rice supply and the crisis was averted.

The military campaign began favourably for the Zamorin. He advanced with a large army into Cochin territory and came as far as Idappalli. The river at Idappalli becomes shallow and fordable over a considerable length. But the approach to it is narrow and near the banks somewhat deep. Up to the ford the Zamorin's army marched without opposition. But there he had to meet a Portuguese captain, Duarte Pacheco, who takes his place in point of military ability, resource and skill, with Clive, de Bussy and Wellington in the history of Indo-European relations. Pacheco had made a careful study of the military topography of the area, in which he was called on to fight and defend, and had made elaborate preparations which were unknown to the Zamorin. He had with him also 100 Portuguese with the best military equipment of the age, besides a large force belonging to the Cochin Rajah. He erected a stockade in the middle of the river, in its fordable part, without either his allies or his enemies suspecting it. When the Zamorin's army approached the ford and encamped on the other side, it found the passage strongly guarded and a caravel with artillery supporting enemy action from the deep end of the ford.

An effort was however immediately made to break through the defence. The Zamorin's plan was to attack with boats on both flanks and try and cut down the stockades by a frontal attack. Both these attempts failed. Pacheco defended the ford with heroic gallantry for over 3½ months, at the end of which the Zamorin retired to his own territory. It is certainly one of the most glorious feats of arms which Indian soldiers under European command have performed in India, and though Portuguese historians celebrate it, Pacheco received neither reward nor honour. Only the Cochin King created him a "Dom."[1] The war was

1) *The grant to Pacheco.*

"We, Kerala Unni Rama Koil Thirumulpad, King of Cochin sovereign of Adavil Cherriveppel, Nedungad, in remembrance that when the Zamorin Rajah attacked us, in Meenam month 679 (Malayalam Era) Pacheco defended us and brought victory to our arms; therefore we grant to him and to his descendants in perpetuity engraved on his shield the five crowns indicative of the five Kings he defeated and seven weapons to indicate the seven battles with the Zamorin. In the handwriting of Chirikandan" (Kerala Pazhama, pages 65—66).

continued in a desultory fashion. The arrival of Lopo Soares with 14 ships gave additional strength to the Portuguese and their allies, and after some abortive pourparlers, Calicut itself was bombarded for two days. After that, Soares attacked Cranganore, the capital of a principality under the Zamorin. Cranganore is situated at the head of the creek and had once been an excellent port. This was the base of the Zamorin's operations against Cochin. Mammali, the admiral of the Zamorin's fleet, made it his chief port and carried on depredatory expeditions against Cochin. Supporting him and waiting for the departure of the Portuguese was the General of Calicut with a large army. The Cochin Rajah informed Soares of these preparations and invited him to attack the Zamorin's sea forces. Soares planned and carried out a surprise attack, destroying many of the Calicut sloops and capturing all the rest. Mammali himself with his two sons died fighting. The Portuguese landed on shore and gave permission to plunder the houses, but as the Nairs made a stout resistance, order was given to burn the town. The Jews who had made Cranganore their headquarters for many centuries considered this the destruction of their own holy city and left that town and settled at Cochin and the surrounding areas.[1]

Besides this fight at Cranganore, the fleet under Lopo Soares carried out another important naval operation. At Pandarini Kollam, the Moors had gathered 17 ships to carry them across to Cairo and Mecca. They had guarded them with guns and kept a

1) "Kerala Pazhama," page 104.

force of 4,000 men to defend it against attack. The ships were laden with merchandise. Lopo Soares attacked it with two caravels and 15 boats. After a long and hard-fought battle the Portuguese gained the victory and the ships were sunk or burnt.

The first round of the contest for the trade of India may be said to end with this. The Portuguese at this time were fighting not for political supremacy or even for the command of the sea as much as for the right to trade with Malabar. The Zamorin who was the most powerful ruler on the coast had opposed it. The Moors whose vested interests were threatened and who were able to realise the significance of the advent of the Portuguese, not only opposed them but used every possible method to drive them out. But the cupidity of the Cochin Rajah, his rivalry with the Zamorin, and his desire to become the leading ruler of Malabar were exploited by the Portuguese who found in him a willing ally and a convenient tool. In the first round of the fight, the Portuguese were not able to establish themselves as a Malabar power. But it became clear that there was no possibility of driving them away from the Indian coast. They had gained the right to trade; and by the relations entered into with Cochin, Quilon and Cannanore, they had secured considerable commercial interests. Neither on sea, nor on land were they the masters; but the Moors, the Zamorin and the other Indian powers recognised, after 4 years of fight, that a new and incalculable factor had been added to the already complicated politics of India.

CHAPTER V

ALMEIDA AND THE NAVAL FIGHT

When Cabral returned to Lisbon the Portuguese King had realised that the problem was either to send a large force and hold the seas or give up the dreams of Indian trade. This, as we saw, was attempted with partial success.[1] But in the meantime, Portuguese interests in India had grown. The policy so far followed was to send out a fleet year by year in the hope that it would be able to destroy Indian shipping and reserve for the Portuguese the sole right of trade. This was soon found impossible; and it was represented to Dom Manuel that without a permanent represent-ative in India with authority to initiate a continuous policy and keep constant watch, even the trade interests in the country would suffer. Manoel Tilles, the factor at Cochin, wrote to the King dated January 8, 1504 that without the appointment of a fully powered officer, the Portuguese in India would not be able to hold their own. The necessity for such organisation was recognised by the King and Dom Francesco d'Almeida sailed to India as the first Viceroy. He was, however, not to take the title without having first built fortresses at Anjediva, Cannanore, Cochin and Malacca. The policy of the Portuguese is made clear by this instruction. It was to build fortresses and hold the strategic centres from which they could com-

1) Faria y Sousa, Asia, page 63.

mand the seas. Each of these fortresses was to be put on a permanent basis with a captain, a staff and a garrison, and the Viceroy was to be the head of the whole organisation. He was also asked to destroy the power of the Moors on the sea, to get the Mahommedan merchants of Calicut expelled and, what is more, to cripple the power of the Sultan of Egypt. What the Portuguese Government discovered early enough was that the power of the Zamorin and his opposition to their schemes had the support of the Sultans of Egypt with whom he was in close alliance. What was of the highest importance, if the power of the Portuguese was to be unchallenged in Malabar, was to break the communications existing between Egypt and Calicut. The necessity for a strategic base at Anjediva arose from this consideration.

Almeida, after erecting a fort at Anjediva, made for Cannanore where also arrangements were made for the immediate erection of a fortress; after this, Almeida took the title of Viceroy. At Cochin, he had to face a political crisis on which the future of the Portuguese policy depended. By one of the many curious customs of the Cochin Royal family, the eldest member took the title of Perumpatappu Muppil and retired into religious seclusion. Thus it is the second man who always ruled as the sovereign. The Muppil died in 1505 and the ruler Unni Rama Varmah, who had welcomed the Portuguese and was in fact their only avowed friend, had now retired from his throne. The heir-apparent, who, according to the matrilineal law in force in the ruling families of Malabar, was the eldest male member counting descent through the female line, was openly against the Portuguese connection. If this prince was to succeed Unni Rama Varmah, the friendly relations established with Cochin would immediately come to an end. The Zamorin as the overlord whose right it was to see that succession laws were obeyed, supported the prince, both from the point of view of policy and that of law. Popular opinion also was strongly in his favour. Even the Rajah did not want to set aside the dynastic law. But Almeida saw that if the Portuguese were to continue their trade relations, decisive action should be taken. After considerable pressure, he made the Rajah agree to supersede the heir-apparent and nominate a more docile prince as the ruler. The new prince was installed and crowned with a golden crown sent from Portugal and he was made to take the oath of fealty and allegiance to the King of Portugal. Cochin thus became not only a subordinate state, but a fief of the Kingdom of Portugal; and its Rajah was henceforth alluded to in correspondence by the Viceroy and others as the faithful servitor of Portugal. Almeida also used the opportunity to secure from the Rajah the right to build a new and strong fortress at Cochin. The immediate result of this arrangement was to plunge the whole country into civil war.

With the Portuguese power thus well established both by the new fort that was built and the complete control established over the Rajah's territory, Almeida took in hand the second part of his instructions, which was the destruction of Arab trade and of the relations existing between the Zamorin and the Sultan of Egypt. His main effort lay in two directions. The first was to close the way through the Maladives, to which line the Arab trade route had been diverted. The Portuguese did not know of the Maladives and to close this line Lorenço Almeida, the son of the Viceroy, was sent with a fleet. He missed the Maladives but reached Ceylon. The second step taken by Almeida was to destroy the naval forces of the Zamorin. The Italian Varthema, who was living in Calicut and who therefore knew the affairs of the Zamorin from internal sources, conveyed to the Portuguese camp the news that there was being equipped at Calicut a large naval force consisting of two hundred small vessels, carrying guns cast by the Italians, which was meant as a convoy for a cargo fleet going to Egypt. The Portuguese navy under Lorenço Almeida met this fleet and, in a grimly fought battle lasting two days, destroyed the Zamorin's ships. It is the superior equipment of the Portuguese navy that gained for Lorenço his victory. The Zamorin, though thus defeated on the sea in the fight against the Portuguese, continued to harass effectively by his ships the trade of those who were their allies. Loyalty was not one of the strong points of the Portuguese captains then in India, and many of them were abandoned to the fury of the Zamorin.

The King of Calicut was also politically active. He was pressing forward a league of Malabar princes against the Portuguese. Those who had allied themselves with the Portuguese were his hereditary enemies, the King of Cannanore and the Rajah of Cochin. The

Zamorin was now able to point out the humiliating servitude to which the Rajah of Cochin had been reduced as an argument to persuade the Rajah of Cannanore to abandon the Portuguese. Other causes also favoured him. The old Rajah of Cannanore who had welcomed the foreigners was dead. The new ruler was not committed to the policy of his predecessor. Moreover, the action of the Portuguese captain Gonzalo Vaz, in violating the safe-conducts issued to the ships of the leading Mahommedan merchant of Cannanore, plundering the cargo and murdering the crew, had caused great anger.

The alliance between the Zamorin and the Kolathiri, as the Rajah of Cannanore is called, was a reversal of traditional policy. But the new circumstances of Portuguese power necessitated it. The Kolathiri laid siege immediately to Cannanore. The fortress held out for four months, though the garrison had to undergo terrible privations. When the entire stock of food and everything edible had been exhausted and the Portuguese were on the point of surrendering, the ships of Tristão da Cunha arrived. The garrison was saved; but the treaty made with Kolathiri showed that the Portuguese realised the danger that lay in the alliance between Cannanore and Calicut.[1]

After putting an end to the trouble at Cannanore, the destruction of the naval power of the Zamorin was again attempted. With the new reinforcements that da Cunha had brought, the Viceroy felt that he was sufficiently strong to attack the Calicut forces at

1) Varthema, page 281.

their base. All the Portuguese vessels on the Indian Seas were concentrated; and with this large force commanded by the Viceroy in person together with Tristão da Cunha and Lorenço d'Almeida, the Calicut forces were attacked and totally defeated.

But the Zamorin had yet another card to play. He invoked the aid of the Sultan of Egypt, with whom he was in alliance, through the Marakkars. The Egyptian merchants in Calicut put pressure on the Sultan, who needed no persuasion as the incessant depredations of the Portuguese were causing Egyptian trade great harm. A fleet was soon fitted up and despatched to the Indian waters under Mir Husayn, an officer of experience and ability. It carried no less than 1,500 men and was equipped with the latest weapons. The idea was to cross to Gujerat and, with the island of Diu as base, operate against the Portuguese fleet. Husayn reached Diu just after the monsoon. The rumour of the Egyptians coming in strength to support the Zamorin had already spread in India. In fact, from the earliest days of their advent to India, the Portuguese always dreaded a strong Egyptian attack. But they had by this time got so far accustomed to this fear that the rumour was not credited. Lorenço d'Almeida sailed north to meet the Egyptian vessels, half disbelieving in their existence. Even when the fleet was sighted, the Portuguese mistook them for the ships of Affonso Albuquerque who was known to be on his way to India from Ormuz.

The two fleets met at Chaul. It was mainly a war of artillery, as the Portuguese attempt to board the

Egyptian vessels was repulsed. After two days of cannonading the Portuguese decided to flee, but the flag-ship of Lorenço d'Almeida was hit and the captain himself was killed. Even up to his last moment, he kept on encouraging his men to fight and it was only after a very hard struggle that the Egyptians were able to board the ship.

The number of Portuguese killed amounted to 140. An almost equal number was wounded. Mir Husayn also lost heavily, but the victory was his. For the time, the Portuguese had lost the command of the sea, and it looked as if they would have to abandon the Indian trade and retire to their homeland.

The superiority of the Portuguese fleet as against the naval forces of the Zamorin lay in better gunnery and more efficient equipment. When it came face to face with the Egyptian fleet which was its equal in every way, the advantage did not lie with the Portuguese. Their easy victories over the Zamorin's ships had made them under-estimate the strength of the enemy and when the guns from Mir Husayn's ships opened an artillery fire directed with accuracy and skill, the Portuguese were surprised. The lesson of the victory was clear to Indian rulers, that without equal equipment and efficient gunnery it was impossible to defeat the Portuguese on the sea.

Almeida realised the gravity of the disaster that had overtaken Portuguese power. He knew that the most urgent necessity was to recover the command of the seas which he had lost. He collected all the ships, men and arms which were available. No time was lost. The

Viceroy started north with this new armada which consisted of 18 ships and 1,200 men. He reached Diu on the 2nd of February, 1509. He had, even before he started, bought off the Governor of Diu, Malik Aiyaz, a Russian convert who had accepted employment under the King of Gujerat. Treachery had thus weakened the Indo-Egyptian force. The Egyptians had only 10 ships as against the Viceroy's 18. As Malik Aiyaz had secretly joined the Portuguese, Mir Husayn's supplies depended upon the 100 sailing vessels which the Zamorin had sent. The battle which ensued on February 3rd was inconclusive, in spite of the tremendous odds in favour of the Portuguese. But the Egyptian ships retired leaving the command of the seas again in the hands of the Portuguese.

The first round in the naval fight was thus over. It was as indecisive in its results as the land fight. The sovereignty of the sea, which the Portuguese claimed, was in a precarious condition. Their authority had not been established in spite of all the fighting that had taken place during the last ten years. The Egyptian adventure showed that with proper handling and efficient gunnery, the Portuguese naval power could be crushed. On land their position was still more precarious. Except the Rajah of Cochin, their old ally who had now been reduced to a servitor, they had neither friends nor supporters on shore. From this perilous position the Portuguese power was saved by the unaided genius, extraordinary resourcefulness and unflinching courage of Affonso Albuquerque, afterwards styled the Great.

CHAPTER VI

ALBUQUERQUE AND THE STABILISATION OF THE PORTUGUESE POWER

Affonso Albuquerque had, along with his cousin, previously visited India in 1503. He was again sent out in April 1506 in command of a convoy consisting of 4 vessels which accompanied a cargo fleet under Tristao da Cunha. Albuquerque was nominated Governor of India from Gujerat to Cape Comorin. The Viceroyalty which was created for Almeida in 1505 included all the possessions and areas over which the Portuguese claimed authority. This was altered in the appointment by provision made in the case of Albuquerque who was nominated Governor only for the area between Gujerat and Cape Comorin, while Jorge d'Aguiar was appointed for the area between the Cape of Good Hope and Gujerat, and Diogo Lopes de Sequiera was to be Governor of the area east of Cape Comorin. All the three Governors were of equal and co-ordinate authority within their respective areas.

Albuquerque commenced his regime as Governor under circumstances which reflect the greatest discredit on the political loyalty of the Portuguese. On his way to India, he anchored at Ormuz and demanded that the King of Ormuz should become a tributary of Portugal. As the King refused this, Albuquerque destroyed the ships in the harbour and landed his men. Thereupon the King agreed to the terms and undertook to pay annual tribute and granted the Portuguese a site on which to build a fortress. A bitter quarrel arose between Albuquerque and his captains on the question of the distribution of the booty. Taking advantage of this quarrel, the ministers at Ormuz refused to ratify the treaty; and when Albuquerque bombarded the town and attempted to blockade it, the captains opened direct negotiations with the enemy and went away to India. Albuquerque had to raise the blockade and retire.

The disobedient captains reached Cochin and represented to the Viceroy, Dom Francesco d'Almeida, that Albuquerque had acted in a high-handed manner and done many things in Ormuz which were irregular and arbitrary. The Viceroy, acting on their advice, wrote to the King of Ormuz disapproving of the action of Albuquerque and promised the King to punish him on his arrival. It should be mentioned here that the appointment of Albuquerque as Governor was to take effect only after the expiration of Almeida's full three years' term of Viceroyalty, and, therefore, the Governor-designate would have been legally under Almeida's orders if he happened to be in Indian waters. Albuquerque, therefore, did not hurry his voyage to the Indian coast and reached Cannanore only on the 5th of December. The Viceroy was on his way to Diu to meet the Egyptian navy and Albuquerque was asked to wait till his return from that expedition. Albuquerque went to Cochin and awaited the return of Almeida. Almeida returned on the 8th of March, but refused to hand over charge on the frivolous pretext that the particular ship on which he had been ordered to return had not arrived. Albuquerque protested against this, but Almeida refused to listen. The faction against the new Governor grew in strength and even drew up a petition asking Almeida not to surrender his charge to Albuquerque. The retired Rajah of Cochin, whom Albuquerque had known personally during his previous visit in 1503 and with whom he was on terms of friendship, was approached by him privately. The Rajah sent word to Almeida that as King Manuel's letter had appointed Albuquerque his representative, goods can be handed over only to him. On this, Albuquerque was accused of intriguing with the Rajah and imprisoned in Cochin and later on sent to Cannanore.

For more than 6 months, Albuquerque was subjected to this kind of indignity. It was only in September, with the arrival of a new fleet under Marechal Dom Ferdinando Cutinho who was a relative of Albuquerque, that Almeida surrendered his authority and left for Portugal—which country however he was not destined to reach, as he was killed along with many others in attempting to plunder an African village. Albuquerque's ill luck did not end with the departure of

1) "Kerala Pazhama", pages 104-106.

2) The full story of the intrigues against Albuquerque which is an illuminating commentary on the Portuguese politics of the time may be read in the Commentaries. It shows the political character of contemporary Portuguese at its worst.

Almeida. The Marechal who had now assumed military and naval command was a rash and reckless warrior to whom political considerations made no appeal. He insisted on an immediate attack on Calicut. Albuquerque had other views. He had already made up his mind that the only safe policy for the Portuguese was to make honourable peace with the Zamorin. To this end he was already in correspondence with the heir-apparent of Calicut. But the Marechal was insistent on attacking the Zamorin declaring that the King had specially sent him out on that specific purpose. Albuquerque agreed half-heartedly. The Cochin Rajah was consulted. The purpose of this was to get the Rajah to attack the Zamorin on the land side as a diversion, and to utilise the Brahmin spies in the Rajah's service to find out the nature and extent of the enemy's preparations.[1]

At the council of war that was held at which the Cochin Rajah was present, the latter reported that the Zamorin was in the interior fighting one of his rebel chieftains, that the garrison in the city of Calicut consisted only of a few hundred Nairs, and that no considerable defence works had been erected on the coast. The fleet started immediately for Calicut and reached that town on the 3rd of January, 1510. Albuquerque landed and captured the jetty. The Marechal was furious that this success did not go to him, and wanted immediately to press on to the palace, conquer the city and destroy it, as he had gaily promised the King. His temerity led to a terrible disaster. In spite of

1) Commentaries, page 54.

Albuquerque's remonstrances, the Marechal marched into the city and overpowered the guards at the palace. The men with him began to pillage and loot and desecrate the whole palace. The news of the defeat of the palace guards roused the Nair militia which soon surrounded the place. Only a small party with Albuquerque at its head escaped. Even they were harassed and pursued up to the sea-shore and the Governor himself was badly wounded. The Marechal, with his chief officers, were cut off from the rest; but he fought like a lion, and ordered the palace to be set on fire. In spite of their heroic efforts, the Portuguese, who had violated the sanctity of the Zamorin's palace could not escape the Nairs. Among those who died on that fateful day, besides the Marechal, were Vasco de Silveira, Lionel Coutinho and Filippe Rodriguez. More than 70 fidalgoes died in the fight. The Marechal's banner remained with the Zamorin's commander and Albuquerque's own flag was captured in his presence by a Nair soldier. The pompous boast of the Marechal that he would bring back to his King a door of the Zamorin's palace ended in the greatest disaster that overtook Portuguese arms in the East.

This defeat decided the course of the Portuguese policy in Malabar. So far the attempt was to subdue the Zamorin and reduce him to the position of a dependent like the Rajah of Cochin. Albuquerque had begun to see even before the disaster at Calicut, that to reduce the power of the Zamorin was an impossible undertaking with the forces at the disposal of the Portuguese, and that the only wise thing to do was to make peace with the Zamorin, abandoning the Cochin policy which, from the time of Duarte Pacheco, the Portuguese had accepted as their own. This defeat also rendered it necessary to find another and more convenient base for naval operations. Albuquerque decided upon Goa as the most suitable place for this purpose. It was impregnable against land attacks and could easily be defended from the sea. The Hindu Kings of Vijayanagar desired to have a port, free from the Mahommedan control, through which they could get their supplies of arms, ammunition and horses, and therefore their Governor, Timoja, helped in the project. The place was easily taken; but Adil Shah, in whose territory it was, roused himself to activity and recaptured it with the help of the Mahommedans in the town. Albuquerque had again failed. He had been driven out of Goa, as he had been out of Calicut. All the three expeditions he had so far undertaken at Ormuz, Calicut and Goa had failed miserably. But Albuquerque's greatness never shone so much as in adversity. He immediately set to work to gather another force. There were many obstacles to be overcome; but his iron will refused to accept defeat, and on October 3rd he started from Cannanore to drive Adil Shah's forces out of Goa. After a very stiff battle, the island was again occupied and defence works were raised immediately with a view to enable the garrison to hold out against any land attack. From the first, Albuquerque had decided to make it the centre of the Portuguese activity in India, and now he took his measures in accordance with this plan.

Almost immediately after settling the affairs of Goa and making arrangements for its development, Albuquerque had to leave for Malacca whence he returned to Cochin only in February 1512. The port of Cochin had been grossly neglected ever since Almeida left India. Albuquerque had other views and was almost continuously employed out of the nominal capital of Portugal in the East, so that almost complete anarchy reigned there. Civil war had broken out in the Cochin state. Unni Rama Varmah, who had retired from the position of the ruler to the titular dignity of Perumpatappu Muppil, died, which meant that the ruler then in authority had to take his place. The Portuguese did not want the continuance of this system; and though the Rajah himself was willing and his people were unanimously insistent, the captain at the Cochin fort decided that the custom was to be abolished and that the Rajah was to continue as ruler. Fearing that he might be persuaded by the members of his family and by the priests, the captain actually imprisoned him within the area under the direct control of the Portuguese. Nuno insisted that the Rajah cannot even abdicate without the permission of Albuquerque. The result of this was a civil war in Cochin, in which the Zamorin intervened to support the claim of the people. Albuquerque himself arrived on the scene and fought for a short time with the Zamorin, but his policy gave him no time to interfere effectively in the internal affairs of the state.

During the short visits he paid to what was even then the chief establishment of the Portuguese in

India, Albuquerque devoted his energies to putting its affairs on a sound basis. When he took charge of Portuguese affairs, not only was indiscipline rife, but the elements of an efficient organisation were absent. In a letter to the King dated 10th of October 1510, he wrote:

> "It appears to me, Senhor, that it is not right to have such a standing as you have at Cochin without an auditor for house and factory, not for a winding up of accounts but that your business be always stimulated and not be trusted to men who say 'I will render an account when I go to Portugal' and meanwhile would have in their possession two or three thousand cruzados or as much as they liked."

Besides this, the officials were all intriguing and fighting against each other. "What reigns here now", he complains in another letter, "is the wish to acquire authority before your Highness, by the defeats of others taking delight in the failures and discomfiture that occur to each other.'"[1]

The affairs of Cochin during the absence of Albuquerque in Malacca had indeed gone wrong. The principal ships of the fleet had been broken up. Many leading people whom the Governor trusted were sent away from Cochin. The blockade of Calicut, which was the principal point of Portuguese policy up to that time, was slackened. From Calicut, six ships laden with cargoes left while the Governor was in Malacca.

---

1) Letter dated 1st April 1512.

"Your factors at Cochin reveal to the King of Calicut the secrets of Portugal and they intrigue with him to cast discredit on your Governor."[1]

In fact, Antonio Reall and Lorenço Moreno were in league with Calicut.[2] The whole system fell into disorganisation. Albuquerque's efforts in Cochin were directed mainly to bring back the efficiency of the factory and to make the fortress stronger.

As the fortress of Cochin appeared to him rather small and of little shelter, he erected a rampart on the side where the ships anchor.[3] It was in the shape of a quadrangle lengthening towards the spot where the ships lie, and came right on to the wall of the fortress itself. It had an entrance towards the sea and another for the ships. Other improvements were also effected in order to make the fortress easily defensible against land attack. He delimited the boundaries between the fortress area and the town, and expelled from the former all who were not Christians. The reason for this act, which Albuquerque gives in a letter to the King[4] is that there were "houses which befriended

1) Cartas, 24—dated November 30th 1513.

2) These two officers hated Albuquerque; but though his subordinates, he was powerless against them. They had the ear of the King. While Albuquerque was away in Malacca, they used their power to persecute all who were in favour of the Governor and wrote to the King misrepresenting the actions of the Governor. They never obeyed his orders. In fact, Albuquerque complained to the King that when after taking Goa, the second time he wrote to the Cochin men "Advising them what it was expedient for them to do in order to strengthen my position in Goa if the Moors were to attack again" he did not receive a reply for three months. (Letter 24, dated November 30th 1513.)

3) Letter dated 1st of August 1512.

4) Letter dated 1st of April 1512.

the outside Gentiles and Moors and these traded in deceiving slaves to rob their masters and escape."

The war with the Zamorin continued its weary course. The injury to Calicut was small. After the retreat of the Egyptians and the defeat of his own navy, the Zamorin changed his tactics. He gave up building ships with which he had hoped to fight the Portuguese, but built instead a large fleet of fast paraoes and kept on harassing Portuguese commerce. Of this new attempt, Albuquerque speaks thus in one of his letters:

> "He had now had 60 caturis made in his land and as the ships of Cochin enter they sally out endeavouring to capture them. Calicut greatly oppressed us with them, because the factor of Cannanore did not dare to send coir or supplies in paqueres and paraoes to Cochin for fear of being captured. The Calicut men would watch on the mountain heights and any atalaya or parao they see coming, they at once pounce upon."[1]

In fact, it was becoming clearer every day to Albuquerque that the fight with Calicut was not in the interests of Portugal, but merely in the interests of the Rajahs of Cochin and Cannanore. "I know," he writes to the King, "why the King of Cochin having 30,000 Nairs and the King of Cannanore having 60 thousand do not go to destroy Calicut; because they want to keep up this dispute (between the Zamorin and the Portuguese) till the end of time. They do not wish to make war, but that we should do so." Albuquerque realised that it was impossible to reduce

1) Torre de Tombo—"Corpo Chronologico", p. 1—Maco 11—Document 50.

the power of the Zamorin by open war. "If your wish is to destroy it by stern war," he wrote, "it will require a fleet always in occupation on her and the fleet of India is not so large that it can be divided into two squadrons."

More, the policy of blockade, by which it was hoped to destroy the commerce of Calicut, had completely failed. Albuquerque informed the King that it was a vain endeavour to guard Calicut in such a way as to cut off its supplies, "because there is much rice in the land, the Dharma Patanam and Cannanore will always supply it in large quantities and this cannot be stopped except by stopping the navigation of Cannanore."[1] "Moreover, when your vessels which sail round Calicut are small and furnished with few hands, they (the Calicut people) rise against them and some aré in the risk of being taken. When they escape this danger, they would withdraw outside. They launch their ships into the sea and load them; and your caravels and small vessels do not dare to send out their boats, while they have a hundred paraoes laden with merchandise around one ship and freight her in two hours and with the right wind the ship goes the round of the sea and your vessels remain at anchor. One goes out of Ponnani, another from Pandarini, some others from Cranganore and others from Chalea while others depart from Dharma Patanam with safe-conducts issued from Cannanore. They have always done navigation and will continue unless you have those ports occupied

1) Torre de Tombo—"Corpo Chronologico", p. 1—Maco 13—Document 106—Letter dated November 30th, 1513.

with some very good ships and some rowing vessels to be close upon the shore."[1]

Realising that the policy of blockade had failed and that the war with Calicut was being continued purely in the interests of the Rajahs of Cochin and Cannanore, Albuquerque opened negotiations with the Zamorin. Though circumstances, as Albuquerque himself admits, were in the Zamorin's favour, the terms which the Portuguese wanted to impose were those of conquerors. These included the permission to build a fortress in Calicut which was to be garrisoned by Portuguese soldiers. As the Governor himself admitted, this meant the destruction of the power of the Zamorin. "If these terms would be accepted," Albuquerque wrote to his King, "you could better bridle and master it and make of Calicut what you desired than by all your campaigns; for it is now 15 years that you have been fighting and yet very little damage has been done."[2] Naturally, the Zamorin, who had by this time fully realised the secret of Portuguese policy, did not consent to this. As a result, Albuquerque began to intrigue with the heir-apparent of Calicut and pressed him to poison the reigning Zamorin. Albuquerque did not hesitate to confess his crime. "I hold it for certain," he wrote to the king, "that the Nampiadiri slew the Zamorin with poison, because in all my letters I bid him to kill the Zamorin with poison, and

1) Torre de Tombo—"Corpo Chronologico", p. 1 Maco 13—Document 106—Letter dated November 30th, 1513.

2) Ibid.

that in a peace treaty I will come to an agreement with him."[1]

The King of Portugal was averse to a treaty with Calicut. He had vowed to destroy the Zamorin, had even sent successive armadas for that specific purpose. A marechal of Portugal, who had publicly undertaken to conquer Calicut for him, had been killed in the city and the Portuguese force driven out. To make peace with the Zamorin without exacting reparations or winning even a victory would be to accept defeat. His point of view was strongly supported by the Cochin clique, Antonio Reall and Lorenço Moreno, who had set themselves to work against the policy of the Governor. They got the Rajah of Cochin to write a long letter to the King of Portugal strongly protesting against the proposed peace with Calicut. He complained that the negotiations were undertaken without consulting him, and that, though the Zamorin is the greatest of their enemies, peace has been made with him without destroying his power. "This peace," he added, "was done for no other reason than that of dishonouring me, and your Highness should not put aside my friendship to take up that of Calicut."

Albuquerque was bound to the new Zamorin, by secret agreement, to make peace; and therefore he did not give the least attention to the Cochin Rajah's complaints, but advised his King to put away his sensitiveness on the matter of making peace with Calicut as it was the Portuguese who were to blame

1) Torre de Tombo—"Corpo Chronologico", p. 1, Maco 13—Document 106. In spite of 15 years' war "Calicut is the largest city in this part of India and the richest" (Cartas).

for the war. He also pointed out that as long as peace was not made with Calicut, foreign intrigues will continue. "It is the hostility of Calicut to us," wrote he, "that makes Venezia so confident of all things of India and put such trust in her former trade; and it is that which makes Cairo equip fleets trusting to eject your ships and men out of India. As long as Calicut continues in its present state, so long will Cairo and Venezia continue to foster their project."

Besides, he promised the King that he would secure by treaty what the Portuguese had so far failed to gain by war. "I do not see what advantage can accrue from the war of Calicut since you do not conquer it. I should state more; if what you wish is to stop her commerce with Mecca you could better effect it by peace than by warfare; I can also obtain all the ginger of Calicut, and I will obstruct all their navigation with Mecca."[1]

It was with these objects in view that Albuquerque entered into negotiations with the new Zamorin who was amicably disposed towards him. The threat of a Turkish invasion of Indian waters, which was one of the alarming rumours then current in India, made him realise the necessity of opening up the Red Sea; and for this purpose he started with a large fleet on February 17th, 1513. The expedition, however, achieved nothing. An attempt to take Aden ended in disaster, and after a fruitless voyage up the Red Sea, the Portuguese fleet returned to Goa in September. The negotiations with the Zamorin, which were conducted by Dom Garcia de Noronha, a nephew of

1) "Corpo Chronologico", p. 1, Maco 22—Document 64.

the Governor, had proceeded satisfactorily, and a definitive treaty was signed, dated Cannanore 24th December 1513.[1]

By this treaty, it was agreed:

1) That the Zamorin should sell to the King of Portugal all spices and drugs there may be in the land;

2) That the Portuguese would pay the usual dues to the Zamorin for the things bought;

3) That if the Portuguese buy horses or elephants they shall pay the usual dues;

4) That the Portuguese would issue safe-conducts to the ships of Calicut.

The other commercial clauses in the treaty laid down, that the Portuguese factor was not to purchase merchandise except in the presence of the King's clerk, so that the King's dues might be collected; that ginger was to be purchased direct from the cultivators and that the price of pepper should be the same as that paid at Cannanore. By another clause, it was agreed "that justice be divided this wise. That any Nayar or native of the land or Moor who shall have any strife or contention with the Portuguese, no harm shall be done to him by the Portuguese, only he shall be taken to the King to be punished and justice done to him. And in the same manner, Portuguese men, when they are found in acts which entail the penalties of justice, the crime being with the Nayars or the natives, they shall be brought to the captain of the fortress for him to punish and have justice done." The Portuguese also undertook to help the Zamorin

1) Corpo Chronologico, p. 1, Maco 13—Document 63.

in his wars as long as they were not against Cochin or Cannanore.

The Portuguese received permission to build a fort near Calicut. The construction of it was immediately undertaken and was placed under the charge of Thomas Fernandez, the master builder. Francesco Noqueira was nominated captain.

Though this treaty was not long in force and war broke out again soon, it is an event of considerable importance in the history of Portuguese relations with Malabar. It marked the failure and consequent abandonment of the policy of conquering Malabar. What was originally attempted was to establish a Portuguese hegemony of Malabar from Cape Comorin to Mangalore, in the same way as Almeida had established it in Cochin. "Cochin is like another of your towns, like Lisboa," wrote the subservient Rajah of Cochin. The aim of the Portuguese was to establish their power on the coast working through the Rajahs of Cannanore and Cochin. This policy could not succeed so long as the Zamorin remained independent; and so Albuquerque looked beyond Malabar and found in Goa a base from which he could command the Arabian Sea. The treaty with the Zamorin also marked the decline in the importance of Cochin and Cannanore. "Do not trouble," wrote Albuquerque, "about the traffic of Cannanore, which is profitless. It has neither port, nor river for the ships, nor galleys, nor merchandise, nor precious stones, nor merchants to trade in your factory." With the founding of Goa, Cochin lost its importance, and the

Portuguese ceased to interest themselves in any very serious way in the politics of Malabar.

The peace, thus established between the Zamorin and the Portuguese, was naturally unwelcome to the Moors. They knew that the previous Zamorin had been poisoned at the instigation of the Portuguese, and that the new King would probably dance to Albuquerque's tune. Though their apprehensions on this score were soon falsified, the Moorish merchants felt aggrieved at the Zamorin's action. "The King of Calicut," bewails a Mahommedan historian, "rolled up the carpet of destruction and pursued the path of friendship with the Feringies."[1]

In the states which were subject to Portugal, Albuquerque interfered forcibly. At Cochin, when the Rajah said that his priests had declared what he was doing to be wrong, Albuquerque quietly replied that he was bound to obey not the priests, but the King of Portugal. At Cannanore, his interference was even more decisive. The Kazi of that place was said to be friendly towards Mussulmans, and Albuquerque asked the King to dismiss him. Naturally enough, the King demurred to such a demand. The Governor immediately drew up a long list of charges, all of which pointed to the same conclusion, namely that the Kazi was not favourably inclined towards the Portuguese. The King promised to enquire into the charges, but Albuquerque insisted on immediate action, threatening to withdraw protection from Cannanore ships if

1) "Nawab Muhabat Khan: Akbar i Muhabat"—Elliot's History.

the King did not yield.[1] The relations with Cannanore continued to be strained during the whole period. The Kazi was supported in his attitude of hostility towards the Governor by Portuguese officers. The trade of Cannanore was much neglected and the factory lost its importance during the time of Albuquerque. Duarte Barbosa was much troubled by this state of affairs, and wrote to the King, thus:

"Let Your Highness order relief to be sent to this factory in merchandise, and by an especial order command that they be unloaded here, because they all pass on to Cochin and they leave us nothing here, nor do they come to remain here three days."[2]

All these representations from various quarters had their effect. Especially, Antonio Reall who had the ear of the King kept up a relentless campaign of hatred and calumny. When the Governor was in Ormuz, orders from Portugal reached Goa that he was superseded, and that Lopo Soares had been appointed instead. Albuquerque, already very ill when he heard of the appointment, died just as his ship was anchoring at Goa on return from Ormuz.

Albuquerque has been deservedly called the Great. He had a high conception of duty, a stern sense of discipline, and an eye for everything political and strategic. He could not have created a Portuguese Empire, because, as will be shown, the Portuguese had neither the resources nor the administrative ability required for it. Nor could he, for any length of time, have put

1) Letter of October 11th, 1512.
2) Volume I of India Office transcript. "Corpo Chronologico" 281.

vigour into their affairs in the East. The importance of his Governorship lies in the general principles on which he founded his regime, and the policy which he initiated. More than even Dupleix or Clive, he was the man who discovered that Indians trained on European methods and using European arms provided a most effective instrument for imperialist aggression. But he was wise enough to realise that Portugal had no resources either in men or in money to cherish any such important territorial ambition in India. What he wanted was to establish a complete monopoly of the Indian trade, to break the combinations that Venice and Egpyt were engineering, and further to place the sea power of Portugal, on which all this depended, on an unshakable footing. The basis of this scheme consisted in having a chain of fortresses from Aden to Malacca, at Ormuz, Diu, Goa, Cannanore, Cochin and Quilon, each one of which would be easily defensible from the sea. But even this required a permanent squadron, and a central base where ships could be repaired, provisions accummulated and central direction maintained. It was for this purpose that he conquered Goa. In a passionate letter to a friend, he described how Goa afforded all the facilities which did not exist in Cochin, how it was large enough to hold a fairly big population, how foodstuffs were plentiful, and how easily it was defensible against attacks.

This scheme of a chain of fortresses meant a regular military force in each place, and a permanent squadron on the seas. But the King was not inclined to send "either arms or men or any equipment of war. He even wanted to withdraw the squadrons." Albuquerque's appeal was for men and money. In every letter, he represented to the King that without adequate forces, the Portuguese would not be able to establish themselves even as traders. He pointed out that "only good strongholds and men will keep the people at peace; by this manner alone will the traffic of merchandise be effected in India without warfare and too many quarrels."[1] He did not ask for much in the way of either men or money. He wanted 3,000 effective soldiers and with that he offered to place the entire trade of India in the hands of Portugal. The only way to avoid war expense and trade lossses in India, in his opinion, was in the maintenance of a good army. "Once more, I repeat," he wrote to the King, "that if you wish to avoid war in India and be at peace with all her Kings, then you should send men and good arms, or that *you* should hold the principal places on the shore of India."

As the supply of men from Portugal could not always be depended upon, Albuquerque decided on the plan of making his Portuguese men marry the Indian women whom he took as prisoners. By this method, he hoped in course of time to bring into existence a body of people to whom could be entrusted the defence of the fortress. Another way in which he hoped to strengthen the Portuguese position in these fortresses was by permitting only Christians to live within the area. In Cochin, all non-Christians were expelled from within the fortress.

1) Cartas, 1st of April 1512.

What Albuquerque had to fight all through his life in India was the intrigue carried on by the Portuguese officials against him. Every factor had the right of communicating directly with the King, and the officials used this privilege in order to misrepresent and calumniate each other. They had no sense of patriotism or loyalty. The factors of Cochin were in communication with the Zamorin when he was fighting against Albuquerque.[1] The officers always lived in disorder, and even the strict habits of the Governor had no influence on them. "Keep away from the letters of your officers," Albuquerque warned the King many times. Moreover, many of the officers had money dealings with the Moors, and were in their pay.

Albuquerque attempted to introduce discipline in their ranks. But he could not succeed. Compared to the quarrel between him and Antonio Reall, that between Hastings and Francis is indeed trivial. He dismissed and sent back to Portugal a good many officers. He fined or otherwise punished those who were guilty of irregularities. He even tried to introduce business habits into the administration. His success was only partial, even during the time of his own authority, for he was never for any length of time either at Cochin or at Goa, but was frequently absent at Malacca or Ormuz. After his supersession, the whole administration again drifted into confusion. Private gain, personal aggrandisement, gross corruption and base intrigue again became the most striking features of the administration of Portuguese affairs in India.

1) November 30th 1513—Letter 24—Torre de Tombo, Part I.

CHAPTER VII

TROUBLE IN CALICUT, COCHIN AND QUILON

By the conquest of Goa, Albuquerque made Portugal one of the minor powers in India, in direct relations with Vijayanagar, and the Bahmini kingdoms. As the main commercial outlet of these prosperous kingdoms, Goa trade had great prospects of development. But from a political point of view, Portuguese power did not in the least advance from the point at which Albuquerque left it. His successors in the Governorship of Portuguese affairs in the East were mostly men interested in amassing wealth by private trade. They had neither political ability, nor loyalty to national interests. Besides, it was not so easy as it was in the time of Duarte Pacheco to win victories against Indian rulers. As Albuquerque confessed in a letter dated November 30th 1513, "the people with whom we wage war are no longer the same; and artillery, arms and fortresses are all now according to our usage." In fact, these conditions effectively prevented any extension of Portuguese authority in India.

The Governor who superseded Albuquerque was Lopo Soares, who had formerly come out to India as admiral of the annual fleet. With him came back all those whom Albuquerque's stern discipline had expelled. The main activity of the Viceroy seems to have been to undo systematically whatever his predecessor had done. Albuquerque had suppressed private trade which was injurious to national interests, and led to the disloyalty of officials. Soares, as soon as he took charge, gave permission to his officers to engage in trade on their own account. After this, he left for an expedition against the Egyptians in the Red Sea, but disaster awaited him at every turn. The heat of the Red Sea took a terrible toll, more than 800 Europeans dying of thirst. All his military adventures ended in failure. The internal administration of Cochin and Goa had also broken down. High officials had tried to engage in plunder and piracy on their own account, which brought on the settlement considerable trouble and loss. One such raid into Adil Shah's territory cost more than 150 lives. Piracy by Portuguese officials was rife on the sea, and the men who took to it never honoured the *Cartas* of the Governors. The "Kerala Pazhama" or the Chronicles of Kerala, which we had occasion to quote before, describes the atrocities of the Portuguese on the seas thus:

> "Besides these cruelties perpetrated on the land, the Portuguese were also responsible for unmentionable atrocities on the sea. The Feringi ships alone did not keep the peace. The Mahommedan ships were the special objects of their fury. Every ship had to carry safe-conduct issued by the Portuguese captain. But even with that they were not safe. The Portuguese seamen demanded heavy bribes and *bakshish*, and if whatever they

asked for was not given the ships would be confiscated."[1]

The only political event of importance in Malabar during the time was the treaty made with Quilon. The Queen of Quilon had invited Vasco da Gama to open a factory there; and in the time of Almeida a factory and a stone-house capable of defence had been built. But when Antonio de Sao was captain a quarrel had broken out which led to the destruction of the factory. The quarrel took place in this manner: João Homem, a captain of the Portuguese fleet, arrived in Quilon and, finding some Mahommedan vessels loading pepper, immediately took possession of them. When the captain left, the people of the town under Bala Pillai, rose up in arms, pulled down the Portuguese factory and set fire to the house. The Portuguese garrison died in the fight. Albuquerque had the good sense to see that the blame lay on the Portuguese and though negotiations were carried on from the Cochin factory, no agreement was reached in his time. After Lopo Soares became Governor, a new treaty with Quilon was made[2] by which the Queen agreed to erect the fort of San Thomé in the same manner and in the same spot, and to compensate for the death of Antonio de Sao by giving to the Portuguese King 500 *bharas* of pepper. The Quilon state also agreed not to export pepper but to sell it only to the Portuguese at the Cochin rates. No dues were to be paid for the use of the port, and the Queen agreed not to receive

1) Pages 164 and 165.

2) Treaty of the 25th of September 1516.

or favour the enemies of Portugal. The treaty with Quilon contained a number of interesting clauses about the local Christians. The Queen was asked to treat them with favour, and it was agreed that the Christian traders in the land were to pay dues to the Portuguese. Freedom of conversion was to be guaranteed.

After this, the relations with Quilon were friendly. The general public of the state was against the Portuguese, and the Queen, realising it, entered into a secret agreement with the captain of the Portuguese factory, Hector Rodrigues. The Portuguese wanted to build a fortress with stone, and, on bribing the Queen with 2,000 silver pieces, permission was given in 1519 without the knowledge of the public. In 1520, a new agreement was made with Quilon by which the captain agreed that private Portuguese traders should pay dues. With the consent and connivance of the Queen who was thus bribed, Rodrigues began to plunder the traders who carried on a great land commerce between Tinnevelly and Kayamkulam. This had the effect of stopping the land route which lay through the Quilon territory and through the Aramboly pass to the East Coast.

The high-handedness of the Portuguese caused trouble in Cochin also. With the permission of the factor of the place, Diogo Mendez de Vasconcellos a Portuguese fidalgo by the name of Gasper de Silva went out to Cochin territory and shot one of the peacocks sacred to a temple deity. The result was that the people of the neighbourhood rose in revolt, and in the riot that ensued 4 of the Portuguese were killed. It had, however, the effect of making the Rajah of Cochin issue a prohibition against the shooting of these birds in his State.

The effect of Lopo Soares' Governorship of 3 years is thus described in a letter of Gaspar Gonsalves to the King[1] "I make known to Your Highness that Lopo Soares in an evil hour came to India, both he and as many of his captains who came with him, because his whole care and mind is no other than traffic and no longer in the service of Your Highness. Before he came, the whole world was at peace; wherever the breath of your Portuguese went it was obeyed; and now you have India all in revolt and no one will obey us and even the most obedient people in India who are the Mukkuvas (low-caste fishermen) want to oust us . . . Now, they attack us, kill us and rob us. And this they say is due to your esteemed and loved Fidalgo of the Household, Antonio Reall of Cochin who it is said is in league with the robbers."

Soares was recalled, and in his stead Diogo Lopez de Sequiera was sent out. Diogo was hardly better than his predecessor and proved an equal failure. His orders were to capture and fortify Diu, in which he failed, and to open up the Red Sea. The importance of this period for Malabar lay in the fight that broke out between the Zamorin and the Rajah of Cochin. The Rajah of Cochin did not like the peace that was established, between his hereditary enemy and the Portuguese, and made successive attempts to embroil them. In 1514,

1) Gavitas Antigas, Maco 6—Document No 51.

he provoked a war with Calicut at Cranganore, and went even to the extent of sending a message to the Zamorin that it was done at the instance of the Portuguese. In this, the Rajah was of course encouraged by Antonio Reall and Lorenço Moreno. But Dom Garcia de Noronha happened to be at Cochin and made it perfectly clear that the Portuguese were not mixed up in the affair.

The motives which led the Rajah of Cochin to try and embroil the Portuguese with the Zamorin are not far to seek. He saw that his ambition of destroying the power of Calicut with the help of the Portuguese, in the vain hope of which he had humiliated himself before his own people by accepting the crown from the foreign King, had no longer any chance of success. Even the material prosperity, which came to Cochin as a result of Portuguese connection, was menaced by the alliance with Calicut. As he complained, "merchants of Calicut all along the coast who had come to ask of me safe-conducts for navigating now proceed to ask for them of the King of Calicut ... All the merchants of the port of Calicut navigate with his safe-conducts." All this meant loss of money and prestige to Cochin. The Rajah was also anxious to wreak vengeance on Calicut for the death of so many of his relatives on the battlefield. His intrigues in 1514 being foiled, the cunning ruler awaited a better opportunity. At about the time that Diogo Lopez was leaving, the Cochin Rajah again declared war on the Zamorin, and asked the Portuguese captain for his help. The Cochin factory sent 40 soldiers, of whom 30 were matchlock men. The Rajah put in the field about 50,000 men and prepared to invade Calicut territory. But the Zamorin forestalled him. The campaign went wholly in favour of the Calicut forces. Though, in a military sense, the war went against Cochin, the Rajah succeeded in embroiling Calicut and the Portuguese. The Zamorin's relations with the Portuguese began to cool down as a result of the help given to Cochin in time of war. The Tofut ul Mujahideen even mentions that in 1517 a perfidious attempt was made against the Zamorin's life. He was invited to the Portuguese fort by the captain with the intention of imprisoning him there; but one of the Portuguese officers, who disapproved of the perfidy, betrayed the plot to him by a signal, and he escaped.[1] Soon, there was again open hostility between Calicut and the Portuguese.

The Portuguese affairs in India were steadily deteriorating. Private gain was the only motive of the Governors, and corruption and intrigue became the chief characteristics of their government. The defences of Cochin had already fallen into decay. Cannanore had been practically abandoned. The incompetent Governors had forgotten the principles and policy of Albuquerque. "One thing I require to remind Your Highness," writes one official to the King, "is that there are no gunners, most of them being shoemakers who know nothing......Likewise arms......we have left our arms where the Moors can take them. The captain scattered the men about and no place was effec-

1) Tofut, page 114.

tively guarded. Naval men were deserting for service in the ships of private traders. In fact, private trade is eating into the very vitals of Portuguese commercial administration. I never witnessed one thing so opposed to the service of Your Highness as this."[1] The private traders, most of whom were of course Government officials, were competing with the royal factories with results that can be imagined. They raised the prices, got the best commodities for themselves and took away from service the ablest seamen. A curious letter, written by Gandangora (Kandankoran) who is described as the Governor of the King of Cochin, addressed to the King of Portugal shows how notorious the matter had become.

"Senhor, I, Gandangora, the Governor of the King of Cochin and overseer of the treasury, on account of the desire I have of serving Your Highness, have resolved upon writing this letter to you in order to give you an account of the things that relate to your service. Your Highness is aware that the merchants of Cochin had always resolved upon serving you with pepper and with other things that may be had. They have now become discontented through the unworthy action of your factors.

"They do not pay regularly; and even more, do positive injury to the traders. Besides, your captains purchase pepper outside at a rate higher than Your Highness pays. The Gentiles will not sell pepper except at that price now. Hence the merchants have besought me to write to Your Highness. Kochali Marakkar,

1) "Corpo Chronologico" Part I—Maco 27, Document No. 69.

who is the principal merchant, declares that Your Highness should send Lorenço Moreno to Cochin in order to serve you as you desire. He enjoys great credit with the Moors as well as others..." The King's revenue was in fact neglected and Governors and other officers cared only for their own profit.

CHAPTER VIII

TROUBLE IN CALICUT, COCHIN AND QUILON

Matters became even worse in the time of Dom Duarte de Menzes who came to India with the title of Governor in January 1522. He was extremely corrupt, engaged in private trade, and openly took bribes. The main activities of the Portuguese at this time were directed against Ormuz and Malacca. The relations with Calicut were very unsatisfactory and for a long time there was trouble between the Portuguese authorities and the Zamorin. Albuquerque had hoped that the blockade of Calicut which the Portuguese ships were not able to undertake successfully as an act of war, could be enforced by a trade treaty which secured for the Portuguese Captain the right of issuing passes. He, himself, states in his letter that this was the object of the peace with Calicut, and that by the treaty he could obstruct all other navigation. But in this Albuquerque did not succeed. The Zamorin's ships and the merchantmen of the Moors refused to take the least notice of the safe-conducts of the Portuguese, and sailed the seas in open defiance. A continuous commercial intercourse was maintained with the Red Sea, and the Portuguese claim of the lordship of the sea was hardly more than a pompous boast.

The result of all this was felt in decreased revenues and diminished prestige. An effort was made by the new King, Dom John, to set matters right, and for this purpose Vasco da Gama who lived in retirement, was commissioned to go out as the Viceroy. Da Gama was the second Viceroy,[1] Almeida being the first. Da Gama, who had been raised to the dignity of the Count of Videguiera, was living in retirement at Evora, having incurred the displeasure of the court. The reason of this estrangement was that Da Gama wanted the lordship of his birthplace and, though the Order of St. Thiago to which it belonged refused to part with it, he proceeded to build a palace and live there. The Order complained to the King, who commanded him to quit the place in 30 days. This was in 1507.[2] The death of Dom Manuel restored him to the favour of the Court and in 1524 he was sent out with the most extensive powers to reform the administration and correct abuses. Twenty years of forced inactivity had altered the character of the man. It was not the hardy adventurer that came out as Viceroy. Even Correa describes him as haughty, proud and disdainful:

"Dom Vasco brought with him great state and was served by men bearing silver maces, by a major-domo and two pages wearing gold neck chains, many equerries and body servants very well clothed and cared for. He also brought rich vessels of silver and rich

---

1) The title of Viceroy was given by royal patent and was supposed to carry almost royal dignity. No one but nobles could sit in the presence of the Viceroy and even grandees could only sit on stools. All others had to speak standing. No one could sit at the same table nor would the Viceroy visit anyone.

Law concerning titles. Memorandum about the Viceroys. "Noticias da India" Vol. I p. 518, Part II.

2) Prestage: Geographical Society's Journal 1925 Jan.

tapestry of Flanders, and for the table at which he sate brocade cloths. They brought to him at table large dishes, as if to the King, with his napkin bearer bringing him the ewer and all the forms of precedence of a King. ...He had a guard of two hundred men with gilt pikes, clothed with his livery...He was a very disdainful man and ready to anger, very rash, much feared and respected. He brought as his secretary Vincento Pegado a noble gentleman who in the office spoke to him with one knee on the ground."

Da Gama's fleet, which consisted of nine ships and five lateen caravels arrived at Goa on the 23rd of September. He assumed the government, without awaiting the arrival of Dom Duarte, and proceeded in a most high-handed fashion. He prohibited private trade and issued a proclamation that if anyone was found to navigate the seas without his permission the ship would be confiscated and the owner banished to Portugal. Correa thus describes his reforms—

"He took away pay and rations from married men who were not to receive them unless there was a war in which they fought or unless they went on board the fleet. He had an enquiry made into the peculations and robberies which the officers had committed in the revenue of the mainland and ordered them all to be arrested and strict accounts to be taken from them. ... He ordered it to be proclaimed, under pain of death and confiscation that any person who had got any of the King's artillery should send and deliver it to the magazine without any penalty, even though they might have stolen it anywhere, and this within the space of one month, after which they would incur the penalty."[1]

After effecting these preliminary reforms, Da Gama sailed for Cochin. Here he was soon made to feel that 25 years of Portuguese effort had not secured for them the mastery of the sea. The Calicut ships sailed everywhere without any acknowledgment of Portuguese authority. Their ships were light and very fast. They appeared in all directions under the very nose of the Viceroy's ships, like street urchins throwing stones at a stranger and running away. Francesco de Mendoca was supposed to be guarding the coast with a fleet of 8 ships; but his vessels were heavy and slow, and the Calicut vessels showed their contempt for him openly. Gama stayed 3 days at Cannanore, where the Kolathiri received him with great honour. He passed Calicut at night and reached Cochin. Almost the first thing he did was to order fast light ships to be built which could fight on more equal terms with Zamorin's vessels. With the help of a Goanese boat builder named Vyne the matter was immediately taken in hand. Before anything much could be accomplished, Gama fell seriously ill, and died in Cochin on the 24th of December 1524. He was buried in the principal chapel of St. Antoni in Cochin, from where his body was removed in 1538; and now he lies buried in the great Cathedral of St. Jeronymus in Belem, which was built almost entirely with the money from India.

Vasco da Gama was hardly a great man. He was neither a great explorer like Magellan, nor a man

1) "Three Voyages". Pages 397 & 8.

of ideas and imagination like Columbus. Of statecraft, he had but little. As between Affonso Albuquerque and himself, there is the difference between a statesman who had the vision of great things and knew how to carry them out, and an adventurer whose ideas were crude and whose imagination was only in the matter of personal luxury. Though money and honours were heaped upon him by Dom Manuel, he was not satisfied and took the order of the King to leave Sine, where he had put forward pretensions of feudal authority, with bad grace. Inordinately vain of his achievement, he was jealous of the good name of other navigators and bore a special hatred towards Magellan.[1] Even in that age of cruelty, his demoniacal inhumanity, of which many examples we have had occasion to give, was such as to create horror. Apart from the discovery of India, for which but little credit as navigator can be given to him as the Cape of Good Hope had already been rounded, and as even the plan of exploring a new way to India was not his, there is nothing that points to any greatness in him. From Melinde he was accompanied by competent pilots who knew every inch of the sea between Africa and Calicut. That he was rash, tactless and overbearing will easily be granted. A mere accident made him the first European explorer to visit India by a route which was not cammanded by the Moors. To compare this event with the achievements of explorers like Columbus, Magellan, Cook or Livingstone is to forget that India was a country which was well known to Europe for

1) "Three Voyages." Introduction p. XXIV.

many centuries before Vasco da Gama, and with which there was uninterrupted commercial intercourse through the Red Sea. The event is pregnant with history, not because a new and unknown country had been discovered but that a way was found for evading the monopoly of the Venetian merchants and the control which the Sultan of Egypt had on the line of communications.

Gama was uncultivated and ignorant. Even Camoens does not hide this. Courage, of course, he had. But that quality he shared with the meanest adventurer that sailed with him. It is indeed strange that this inhuman, greedy and uncouth sailor should have, in the popular imagination of Europe, become one of the heroes of his age, greater in the estimation of his countrymen and the world than Henry the Navigator, Affonso Albuquerque, Magellan, Camoens or Duarte Pacheco.

Da Gama's third visit to India as Viceroy was merely an unimportant incident. He was not able to check the decay that had set in. His successor was Dom Henrique de Meneses. His period of government is important for Malabar, because during his time Malabar became a scene of warfare, and the struggle for naval supremacy reopened.

The Zamorin, who was bribed by Albuquerque to murder his uncle, was dead. The traditional policy of the Kings of Calicut was to encourage trade with Egypt, Cambay and Arabia, and to maintain the proud title of the Lord of the Seas. The Portuguese pretensions of being sole masters of maritime traffic was a sufficient cause of trouble. Nor did the rulers of

Calicut look with favour on the small fortress that the Portuguese had built on the shore of Calicut. As was to be expected, the trouble, which was brewing for a long time, came to a head in the matter of rival claims on the sea. In 1524 the leading Mahommedan merchants of Cochin, Ahmed Marakkar, his brother Kunjali Marakkar and their maternal uncle Mahommed Ali Marakkar, left Cochin because of the oppression of the Portuguese, and went and settled down at Calicut. Enraged by this, Henrique de Meneses and Lope Vaz de Sampayo attacked Ponnani,[1] the naval station of the Zamorin, and stormed it. In this campaign the Portuguese secured the help of the Arayan of Procaud, the naval commander of the Chief of that place. Dom Henrique de Meneses, who suspected the Arayan of half-heartedness in the latter part of the campaign, ordered his men to shoot his ally---the Arayan was in fact seriously wounded. On account of this treacherous conduct of the Portuguese, Procaud declared war. After much desultory fighting on the sea, the Arayan was defeated in 1525, and Procaud itself was plundered in 1528. In the plunder the Portuguese took, besides large quantities of gold and silver, a number of cannon and 13 vessels.

The naval war with the Zamorin was all this time going on without any decisive engagement. After the destruction of Ponnani by Francesco d'Almeida in 1507, the Kunjali Marakkars, who were the hereditary admirals of the Zamorin's fleet, had shifted their head-

1) Faria I, 284.
2) Faria I, 292.

quarters to Kottakkal. Under Kutti Ali, in 1524, a large and effective fleet took the sea and did great damage to Portuguese trade. Lope Vaz de Sampayo came into action against Kutti Ali of Cannanore but the results were not decisive. Kutti Ali's prowess on the sea was such as to strike terror into the hearts of the Portuguese; and for over two years he practically cut off all connection between Cochin and Goa. Finally, the Governor made a supreme effort to destroy his power, and in a fight in 1528 Kutti Ali was taken prisoner. This however did not affect the growth of Zamorin's sea power; for Kunjali II, the son of Kutti Ali was soon to follow his father's footsteps with greater success.

On land also, the fight was carried on with vigour. The Zamorin's forces besieged the Calicut factory. Dom Joao de Lima who was the factor of the place defended it stubbornly, but the Zamorin pressed the enemy hard. Antonio Rabello, who took part in the fight, describes it thus in a letter to the King.[1] "On one side of the fortress they made deep trenches and ditches and placed artillery, and on the other sides Nairs made entrenchments. They bombarded the fort for many days, but perceiving that they were not causing much damage they erected flat mantlets. One day Captain Dom Joao ordered us to sally out against one of these, and we set fire to it. The enemy also erected wooden castles and filled them with musketeers. The Nairs then made an attempt to starve the fortress by setting all their forces on the side of the sea so as

1) "Corpo Chronologico." Part I Maco 33. Document 59.

to prevent disembarkation and the entry of supplies. Message was sent to the Governor who at once despatched Christoam Infante with two caravels and supplies for the fortress. He landed at fall of day between the two towers with 30 men.......The Governor himself came with all his fleet to Calicut where he remained for 15 days holding a council as to whether he should land. He resolved upon getting down and sent Francesco Antonio da Silviera with 400 men. This was accomplished only with great difficulty because the boats could not be brought near the shore. A council was then held to decide as to the best way of attacking the entrenchments. The plan adopted was to give signal to the fort for a sortie to clear the shore and then the captain in chief was to land. This was successful—the siege was raised."

Negotiations were immediately opened by the Zamorin, but they came to nothing as the Portuguese wanted the fortress to be rebuilt. War was therefore renewed, and the Portuguese were forced to abandon their foothold on Calicut land and withdraw. The effort to subdue Calicut by building a fort in the capital had failed. For the fourth time during 25 years the Portuguese had to acknowledge defeat and to withdraw after prolonged conflict with the Zamorin. It is generally claimed by Portuguese historians that the war inflicted heavy damages on the King of Calicut. As Rabello points out, it is true that they were able to sink a number of Calicut ships, but the losses of the Portuguese were greater. The income from *cartas* alone was 1500 cruzados every year. That, together with the very profitable trade that was carried on, was lost to the Portuguese. "The whole evil came through us," bewails Rabello.

Dom Henrique de Meneses died in 1526, and was succeeded by Lope Vaz de Sampayo as Governor. The war with the Zamorin continued almost exclusively on the sea. Under the leadership of Kutti Ali, who was assisted by the Arayan of Procaud, the fight went on as mentioned before; but in 1528 Kutti Ali was taken prisoner, and Procaud was captured and plundered. The Zamorin, however, fitted up another fleet under Pachachi Marakkar a relation of Kutti Ali. With him was sent Kunjali, the son of Kutti Ali, who was destined to become the greatest of the Zamorin's admirals. A portion of the fleet was under the command of Ali Ibrahim. The first attempt of the combined fleet was against the Portuguese settlement in Ceylon. In Ceylon, the quarrels between the reigning King Bhuveneka Bahu and his brother Mayadunna had helped the Portuguese to re-establish their authority on the pretext of helping the ruler. The Zamorin took the side of Mayadunna, and his fleet under Pachachi Marakkar appeared at Kotte. The fight between the naval powers in the Ceylon seas continued till 1535, when the Portuguese had to withdraw their forces to face a new and more powerful enemy, who made his appearance on the Indian seas—the Turkish Admiral Suleiman Pasha.

Lope Vaz de Sampayo was extremely high-handed in his dealings with his subordinates. He imprisoned the Rajah of Cochin, interning him in his own palace.

The trouble with Cochin, leading to the imprisonment of the Rajah, arose from that ruler's claim for port dues. In a letter to the King of Portugal[1] he complained:

"Albeit that I cannot deny having received many favours of Your Highness, nevertheless I cannot desist from reminding you of this favour guaranteeing me of the duties from the port of Cochin, on all the junks, ships, and all other things whatever that may come here from Malacca, Bengala and any other part. These dues are not at present paid and I do not dare to grieve any one by demanding them, albeit that these duties belong to me as they belonged to my ancestors. Your Highness has also agreed that any fidalgo, captain or any one else of any rank who should bring goods here should pay me the said duties because it is these men who have in their hand most part of the trade. Let your Highness write to the Captain in Chief, the Controller of the Exchequer to have it done, because unless they pay me I could not sustain a great part of my expenditure."

The Portuguese authorities in Cochin steadily refused to give the Rajah's dues to him on one pretext or another. Affonsio Maxia, the Controller, in spite of pressure from officials, refused to yield on this point. Writing to the King of Portugal on January 15, 1530, he states:

"Antonio Saldana when he arrived here at once came to ask me to give up to the King of Cochin the duties owing to him. I did not want to tell him before the

1) "Corpo Chronologico," Part I. Maco 52, Document 23.

factor and the clerk of the treasury that this had nothing to do with him. I asked him to desist from arguing, but he continued to bring messages from the King of Cochin until I told him secretly that I did this by commission from your Highness."

With the other rulers, in alliance with Portugal, he was equally tyrannical in behaviour. His position as Governor was, however, irregular, as the successor to de Meneses, by the order of the King, was Pero Mescarenhas, who at that time was away in Malacca. In the meantime new orders were received from Lisbon appointing Lope Vaz as Governor. Though tyrannical and arbitrary, he was a good soldier. He kept the fleet in a high state of efficiency, and the forts under repair and with ample munitions. He was superseded by Nuno da Cunha.

Almost the first act of the new Governor was to reopen the war with the Zamorin on the sea. Diogo de Silveira with thirty ships was ordered to engage the Zamorin's fleet and to maintain a close blockade of the Calicut coast. This he did most effectively, capturing no less than 27 large ships richly laden with merchandise. He also suggested that a fortress at the mouth of the Beypoor River at Chaliyam was necessary if the naval power of the Zamorin was to be annihilated. The Beypoor River runs through the middle of the Zamorin's territory dividing it into equal halves. If a fortress and naval station could be established at the mouth of the river, lighter craft could operate in the interior and harass the internal trade of the Zamorin. The feudatory Chief who owned the area around Chaliyam was the Rajah of Tanur who was favourably disposed towards the Portuguese. Negotiations were opened with him. After some hesitation the Chief of Tanur agreed, and the Portuguese built a fortress in which a strong garrison was stationed. The best available artillery was brought to this place and no pains were spared to make it impregnable.

The strategical value of the Chaliyam fort was such that it was like a pistol held at the Zamorin's throat.[1] It affected his whole trade and threatened his communications, in case he attacked Cochin. It gave the Portuguese a base from which they could carry war into the Zamorin's territory. Zeinuddin, who had an eye for military considerations, declares that the Portuguese official who negotiated the agreement with the Rajah of Tanur was a "master of the greatest subtlety, cunning, and capable of deep strategem." For 40 years the effort, towards which the Zamorin directed all his strength, was to expel the Portuguese from this port, in which undertaking he succeeded only in 1571.

The naval fight continued. Kutti Ahmed Marakkar, who was the leading captain on the Calicut side, was killed in 1531, and his place was taken by Kunjali II, whose ability and knightly manners evoked admiration even from the Portuguese writers. Kunjali had learnt naval warfare in the new school. He, therefore, had no hesitation in paying the Portuguese back in their own coin. Whenever he captured a Portuguese ship—and he captured no less than 50 in one year—he

1) See Cochin Rajah's letter dated 1533, Dec. 18. "Corpo Chronologico" Part I Maco 52. Document 23.

slew the entire crew. The result was that warfare in Malabar waters was intensified, and the Portuguese as well as the Indians suffered heavy losses.

Events were, however, taking a new turn. Portuguese power at this time was faced with a hostile combination, more dangerous than any it had to face before. An alliance was made between Cambay and Calicut, and an effort was made to obtain the help of the Turks, who had now become masters of Egypt. In pursuance of a common scheme the Zamorin attacked the Portuguese in Cranganore. With the help of the Rajah of Cochin, the fort was defended but the Portuguese, in spite of their advanced position at Chaliyam, could not take the offensive against the Zamorin.

Martim de Sousa, who was in charge of the Malabar squadron, realised that if the Zamorin's power for offence was to be seriously curtailed the enemies nearer Cochin, on whom the Calicut Ruler depended for support, should first be subdued. The classic reply of the Zamorin to any offensive directed against his State was to get the Rajah of Idappalli who, from his position on the rear of Cochin and from his command of the nodal points, was a standing menace to the safety of the Portuguese and their ally, to make a diversion from his side. De Sousa decided, therefore, to attack the Rajah of Idappalli. A powerful force under Antonio Brito invaded the territory of that Brahmin Chief and laid the country waste. His capital was sacked, and the Ruler, himself, was reduced to great straits. The Zamorin immediately came to his rescue. With a large force he started south. At the ford of

Kumbalam, which was defended by a Portuguese force, his army was held up. To divert the attention of the Portuguese and to get them to withdraw their forces from Idappalli, the Zamorin's fleet under Kunjali appeared before Cochin and began successfully intercepting Portuguese convoys. This ruse succeeded as Martim de Sousa had to withdraw all his forces from land in order to meet Kunjali. Idappalli Rajah was saved, and the Zamorin withdrew.

The sea fight continued. Kunjali and his fleet had rounded Cape Comorin and attacked the Portuguese establishment at Nagapatam. But there they were overtaken by a Portuguese squadron and the fight went against the Calicut forces. Kunjali himself had to escape in disguise to Calicut. In 1537, however, a new Calicut fleet appeared on the sea, which conducted a very successful campaign against Portuguese merchant vessels. Martim de Sousa tried to chase the vessels, but the Marakkars eluded him, and continued their adventurous career on the sea inflicting serious loss on the trade as well as the naval prestige of the enemy. It was only on the 20th of February 1538, that Martim de Sousa was able to fight a great battle with the Marakkars and to get the sea cleared for a short time. The success was in the nick of time, because the Portuguese had soon to mobilise their whole strength to meet the Turkish expedition under Suleiman Pasha Al Khadim.

It was early in 1537, that Suleiman Pasha, the Turkish Governor of Egypt, began the preparations for an attack on Portuguese power in Indian seas. The instructions which the Pasha received from Sultan Suleiman the Magnificent were as follows.[1]

"You who are the Beglerbeg of Egypt, Suleiman Pasha immediately on receipt of my orders will get ready your bag and baggage and make preparations in Suez for a holy war and having equipped and supplied a fleet and collected a sufficient army you will set out for India and capture and hold those Indian ports: cutting off the road and blocking the way to Mecca and Medina you will avert the evil deeds of the Portuguese infidels and remove their flag from the sea."

The arrival of Suleiman Pasha off the Gujerat Coast made the concentration of all available Portuguese ships necessary to ward off that attack. The Turkish adventure, however, proved abortive, as Suleiman merely made a naval demonstration and returned to Egypt without actually engaging the Portuguese.

The retirement of the Turks came as a great blow to the Zamorin. Fifteen years of uninterrupted struggle had exhausted his treasury. Not one but four fleets of his had been sunk, and the trade of Calicut was languishing. The Portuguese had established themselves at Chaliyam which gave them a unique position to carry on the war against him. Moreover, his old enemy, Unni Rama Kovil, the roi faineant of Cochin who had been placed on the throne by Almeida, had died in 1587. As a result, the Zamorin agreed to negotiate a new treaty of peace. Kutti Ali, a relation of Kunjali the admiral, was sent to Goa, where he was received with pomp by the Viceroy, Garcia de

1) "Tarjuma Nuzhat as Sunna"-British Museum MSS. Add 7846 pp. 66a.

Noronha, who had in the previous year succeeded the Governor Nuno da Cunha. Garcia de Noronha, who was the third Portuguese Viceroy in the East, was a nephew of Affonso Albuquerque and had served with him in India. The treaty was negotiated between the Zamorin and Dom Alvaro, who was sent to Calicut, on the basis of a preliminary set of terms which the Zamorin had sent through his ambassador.

The treaty was signed on the Galleon S. Mathews at the bar of Ponnani on the first of January 1540. The transcript dated December 6, 1539[1] runs as follows:

"Dom Garcia de Noronha, of the Council of the King, our Lord, Viceroy, Captain in Chief, and Governor of India, makes known to all. . . . that the Zamorin sent him ambassadors by whom his desire for peace was communicated. He sent Dom Garcia notes on which he was prepared to act. These notes were read in the Council of Captains and other notables and they agreed that peace should be made on that basis. As he (Dom Garcia) had S. Mathews made ready to go to Calicut but fell ill Dom Alvaro de Noronha his son, Dom Joao de Castro, his brother-in-law (later Viceroy), Pedro Lopez de Sousa, Captain in chief of the fleet and Dr. Pernao Rodrigues de Castillo Branquo, Controller of the Treasury and Joao de Coasta as secretary were sent to negotiate. The following letter was addressed to the Zamorin:

"I beseech as a favour of the most high and very powerful lord the Zamorin King of Calicut that whereas I am unable owing to my indisposition to go

1) Tombo of the State of India. Folio 216.

personally to effect the said peace that he should establish it with the aforesaid . . . and swear to them as is his custom because I shall keep to and fulfil as entirely as though this had been made by me."

It was agreed by the treaty—

1) that the Zamorin should sell all the pepper that might be in his lands to the King of Portugal at the rates prevailing in Cochin, and that ginger in the land should also be sold to the Portuguese at 92 fanams per *bhara*, the price including the dues which the Zamorin should have;

2) that the Zamorin should be entitled to send to Portugal pepper to be sold at the same price as that at which the Portuguese King sold his. For each 100 *bharas* which the Portuguese King sells the Zamorin should be entitled to send 3½ *bharas* of his own, bought with his money to be sold in Portugal at 15 cruzado per quintal. It was further agreed that the money so made should be sent back to the Zamorin by the Portuguese King in the shape of merchandise so that "he could double his money;" and that the merchandise should be quicksilver, vermillion and coal;

3) that the transportation, sale etc., of the Zamorin's pepper was to be entirely at the risk of the Portuguese King. The Zamorin was to lose nothing if the ships were damaged, or the goods lost; and

4) that a part of the Portuguese merchandise should always be sold at Calicut, in order that the Zamorin may have the customary dues.

The Zamorin also agreed to accept from the Portuguese *cartas* for the navigation of Moorish vessels. He agreed not to make war on the friends of the Portuguese (meaning the Rajah of Cochin), but if he did make war, the conditions of the treaty were not to be disturbed.

This treaty secured for the Zamorin great advantages. It gave him a settled income from Portuguese trade without any risk, and it revived the trade of Calicut. He also secured for himself complete freedom of action against the Cochin Rajah. The Portuguese on their side also gained considerably. The Zamorin agreed to accept the *cartas* for Moorish ships, and to sell pepper and ginger exclusively to them. There is no doubt that considerable relief was felt by the Portuguese at the satisfactory conclusion of this treaty. The war with the Zamorin had not gone in their favour, and had caused them great loss both in trade and in men. Peace with the Zamorin meant for them freedom of action with other Malabar Princes, as the Cochin Rajah and others soon discovered.

The first to feel the effect of this treaty was the Rajah of Procaud, whose capital had been plundered in 1528. The Rajah, with the help of one of the Karappuram Kaimals[1] attacked a Portuguese squadron and captured it. Dom Christovao da Gama immediately demanded satisfaction of the Rajah, who disclaimed all responsibility and declared it to be the work of the Kaimal.

1) Barons who divided among themselves the peninsula between the backwaters and the sea.

Da Gama attacked that Chieftain's territory and laid it waste. The Kaimal was slain in the fight. The Rajah of Procaud, considering discretion to be the best part of valour, made a treaty of friendship and alliance with the Portuguese.

Estava da Gama who was Governor for two years (1540-1542) was succeeded by Martim Affonso de Sousa, who shares with Duarte de Meneses the odium of being the worst Portuguese Governors who came out to India. He reduced the plunder of temples and sacred cities to a system and made it worse by hardened and inhuman cruelty. Even in 1540, two years before Martim de Sousa came to India, the King of Portugal had issued orders that all Hindu temples in Goa were to be destroyed. De Sousa went a step further. He considered it evidently a part of his duty to his Christian sovereign, that the temples of the idolaters, wherever found, should be razed to the ground, and their hoarded wealth plundered, in order to fill the purse of Christian adventurers. The following description from Whiteway (taken from Barroes) pictures the activity of the new Governor in this direction.

"The Conjeevaram temples stand some 40 miles inland from Madras and were, at the time of which we are writing, in the territory of the Rajah of Vijayanagaram. They were visited regularly by the Rajahs themselves....Kanchi, as it is called in sacred writings, is one of the holy places of India...Enriched by the annual stream of pilgrims and endowed by the munificence of the Hindu Rajahs of Vijayanagaram, the wealth of the temples was very great.

De Sousa, in the rains of 1543, organised an expedition to pillage the temples. As such an attack would have roused the whole coast, preparations were made to carry off the remains of St. Thomas (supposed to be buried at Mylapore near Madras). The fleet which sailed early in September was scattered and delayed by a storm. Though the preparations were made secretly, enough had leaked out to make the Rajah of Vijayanagaram uneasy. When, therefore, the Portuguese rounded Cape Comorin, they found so large a force collected, that any attack was out of the question. Therefore, De Sousa returned with his forces to Kayamkulam.

On this coast, between Cochin and Quilon, the Portuguese had been settled for over 40 years, and they depended upon the goodwill of the residents for the supply of the merchandise which was the bait that drew them to the East. This did not prevent De Sousa from leading an expedition to attack the temple of Tevelakkarai, a few miles inland, which local information reported to be enormously wealthy. There were two Jungadas (companies) attached to this temple; but one of the captains with almost all the guards had gone to the south when the movements of the Portuguese first attracted attention. An offer of £ 12,000 down failed to turn the Governor from his intention and before nightfall the temple was reached. The building was of the usual design, surrounded by a wall with a few straw huts outside. The Governor and his immediate following went inside the temple and shut the door; those outside the building passed a miserable night, a prey to every imaginable horror—the fall of a shield nearly caused a stampede. Inside, the Governor and his friends spent the time in torturing the Brahmins of the temple and in digging up the floor. It was never known exactly what was found, a gold paten worth ₤50 was all that was ever shown; but as two barrels of matchlock powder were emptied, and the barrels passed in, and as afterwards they each required 8 slaves in relays to carry them, scandal was busy. When, in the morning, they started on their return journey, a Nair, dressed with scrupulous care, with all his ornaments, followed by 10 or 12 others, flung himself on the Portuguese ranks. It was the remaining Jungada, with his relatives whom he could collect, who thus tried to wipe out by their deaths the stain upon their honour. During their retreat, the Portuguese were harassed by the country people, and suffered a loss of 30 killed and 150 wounded; but on the way, they sacked another temple whence they obtained some small amount in silver coins to distribute among the soldiery."

De Sousa's treachery also brought him into conflict with the Rajah of Chirakkal—the oldest ally of the Portuguese in India. Abu Bakr Ali, a nephew of the great Mammali Marakkar of the time of Albuquerque, was foully murdered by Bastio de Sousa, a relative of the Governor, who was sent to Cannanore for the purpose of extorting money from him. Of the merchants of Cannanore, the Mammali family was the richest and most influential, and the murder of Abu Bakr Ali was an outrage equalling in brutality the action of Gonzalo de Vaz in murdering on sea, in defiance of a Portuguese safe-conduct, another nephew of Mammali. The result was an immediate declaration of war by Cannanore.

Martim de Sousa also negotiated a new treaty with Quilon on the 25th of October 1544.[1] It is declared that the treaty was negotiated with "the Adhikari Kaimal, Cate Nambiar, and with the Pillas, Nairs and Rulers of the said land." The treaty provided that in the event of a Portuguese or a native Christian being guilty of any crime he was to be sent to the captain for trial and punishment. The Portuguese were to be exempt from all dues. The Church of St. Thomas was to be specially protected. The Portuguese on their side, promised not to kill cows in Quilon territory.

In 1545 Dom Joao de Castro came out as Governor. The new Governor made peace with Cannanore and, in fact, generally tried to set right the mischief done by his predecessor. The importance of his governorship (which was later on converted into a Viceroyalty) lay in the development of Portuguese religious policy. For some time past, the Portuguese authorities had been thinking seriously about the problem of Christianising those areas over which they had control. Their lack of power alone stood in the way of systematic persecution and wholesale conversion, as we shall show later. In the time of Joao de Castro the matter was taken in hand in earnest. The King of Portugal was especially anxious, and wrote to him a letter dated Lisbon, 8th of March in which he asked the Viceroy

1) "Tombo de Estado da India" Fol. 37.

to take the most vigorous steps to put down heathen practices.

He also wrote that the King of Cochin should be asked to grant privileges and show favour to Christians.[1] An attempt was made even to convert some of the Malabar Rajahs. The only success they had was with the Rajah of Tanur, who was a rebellious feudatory of the Zamorin. This Chief had sold Chaliyam to the Portuguese hoping to benefit by the Portuguese connection at the expense of the Zamorin. When negotiations about his conversion were going on, the Viceroy, Dom Joao de Castro died. In the time of Garcia de Sa, the Rajah was again pressed, and a Jesuit, by the name of Antonio Gomez, was sent to instruct him in the Faith. He went to Goa, and was there admitted with great pomp into the Church. But this apostacy was of short duration. After a few months of trial, when he found that the hoped for benefits did not come, he returned to the religion of his ancestors.

For ten years now there had been peace between the Zamorin and the Portuguese. The friendship of the Zamorin had given the Portuguese freedom to attack and reduce the smaller Rajahs of the coast; and this high-handed policy caused hostilities to break out once again between the Zamorin and the Portuguese, who as usual put the Cochin Rajah forward to fight their battles. The cause of war was a dispute which arose between the Rajah of Vadakkumkur—the Nair Chief who controlled the market of pepper produced in the hills in the interior—and the Rajah of Cochin.

1) "Life of Castro." P. 46.

When the dispute came to a head, the Vadakkumkur Rajah offered to abide by the arbitration of the Portuguese Captain. The Cochin Rajah also was not averse to this; but Francesco de Silva thirsted for war, and insisted that if the Vadakkumkur Rajah did not surrender unconditionally he would invade the territory. War broke out in 1550. In the first battle that ensued at Vaduthalai, the Vadakkumkur Rajah died on the field, and his troops, as a result, fled in confusion. Encouraged by this the Portuguese marched on, entered his capital and set fire to the palace. The defeated army had, however, rallied and attacked the Portuguese force with vigour, which in turn fled with much loss, and the captain, Francesco de Silva was himself killed. The Vadakkumkur army followed up this advantage, invaded Cochin and ravaged the territory. The Portuguese and their ally, the King of Cochin, had to take refuge in the fort.

The action against Vadakkumkur, who was a feudatory of the Zamorin, brought the King of Calicut into the field. Even the Rajah of Tanur, who was a friend of the Portuguese and had become a temporary Christian, marched at the head of his forces at the call of the Zamorin. The Captain of Cranganore blocked his way to the Cochin territory, but, by marching through the lands of the Chief of Kavalappara who was one of his generals, he was able to reach Trichur. All his important feudatories, including the Rajah of Kurumburnad, the Nambidi of Venganad, the Chief of Kavalappara and the Rajah of Mangat, were with him. The Zamorin's army occupied Vaduthalai, and though for a short time the Portuguese established a blockade they were unable to make any impression. The Governor, Georges Cabral, was in the meantime superseded and his successor, Dom Affonso de Noronha, made no effort to press the war to a conclusion. The Zamorin's forces maintained their supremacy on land. The following is the reference that Diogo Botelho makes about this war in his letter to Baron d'Alvito: "There was war with the King of Calicut. The reasons were the quarrel between the King of Cochin and the Zamorin and because pepper was not coming through. Enrique de Sousa was the Captain at Cochin but Manuel de Supedveda was sent from Goa with orders to relieve him. Supedveda immediately proceeded to attack Vaduthalaa and opened negotiations with the Rajah of Tānur who was the ensign-in-chief of the Zamorin."[1]

The history of the Portuguese after the time of Dom Affonso Noronha is a tale of ineptitude and corruption. The war on the sea continued, for, though by the treaty of 1540 the Zamorin had agreed to take out the safe-conducts, the conduct of the Portuguese in disregarding these on flimsy pretexts soon gave rise to quarrels. Luiz de Mello, who was the captain of the fleet, endeavoured unsuccessfully to come to action with the Calicut fleet. A squadron of the Zamorin's fleet with 15 vessels attacked Panicale which was under the command of Manoel Rodriques. The Portuguese were put to flight, and the town was occupied and plundered by the Calicut men. Under Kunjali Marakkar the Calicut forces began to take to guerilla

1) "Corpo Chronologico." Part I. Maco 84. Letter dated July 15, 1551.

warfare on the sea, attacking convoys, destroying merchant ships and generally harassing the trade. These tactics met with much success. Kunjali avoided the Portuguese fleets and fought pitched battles only when he was forced to do so by circumstances. Luiz de Mello was, therefore, unable to get the Calicut fleet into action till 1558. Kunjali had the support of the naval commander of Cannanore, whose ruler, though traditionally the ally of the Portuguese, had owing to the rudeness of Dom Payo de Noronha, become their inveterate enemy.

The battle was fought off Cannanore. The flagship of Kunjali was sunk in the fight, and the Portuguese captured three other ships. Though the losses of the Calicut fleet were thus heavy, the victory of de Mello was no more than nominal, as nine out of the thirteen Calicut vessels retired unpursued and continued their depredations. De Mello, who had gone to Goa to celebrate the victory, had to return immediately to cope with this danger. This time he came determined to destroy altogether the offensive power of the Zamorin's fleet on the sea. The Viceroy supported him in this, and gave him an additional force of 27 ships and 600 men. With this armada he appeared on the Malabar coast. This time the Portuguese Commander decided on a change of plan. The traditional strategy of the Portuguese was to chase the Malabar fleet and force it to fight a decisive action. This time De Mello decided to split up his forces and guard the main river mouths with a view to intercepting all egress and ingress. The Commander, himself, sailed up and down in his flagship, burning cities and ravaging the coast mercilessly. This policy met with considerable success and was carried on vigorously in 1559 and 1560.

Luiz de Mello was recalled in 1560 and the Malabar ships again appeared on the sea. The war with Cannanore was still going on, and the Zamorin's ships were helping the Kolathiri Rajah in harassing the enemy's transport. Dom Francesco de Mascarenhas who was sent by the Viceroy to bombard Cannanore and carry on the fight vigorously was attacked by the Malabar vessels, and one of the ships commanded by Jeronymo de Meneses had to fly hastily before the enemy. In reply to this the Viceroy, Conde de Rodondo, fitted up a fleet under a captain by the name of Domingas de Mesquita with express orders to kill all the men whom he could capture on the Malabar coast. De Mesquita, who was charged with this task, accomplished it with a very easy conscience. He was able, within the next few months, to capture 24 vessels, the men in which, in obedience to Viceregal orders, were either beheaded or sewn in sails and thrown overboard. It is estimated that no less than 2,000 men suffered this cruel fate. The Zamorin complained to the Governor Joao de Mendoça, but he refused to take any action. Enraged at this condonation of the barbarities perpetrated against his subjects, the Ruler of Calicut denounced the treaty of 1540 and declared war.

The hostilities between Cannanore and the Portuguese, which had started in 1558 as a result of Payo de Noronha's rudeness, were still going on, and with the Zamorin openly on the side of the enemies, the Portuguese in Malabar were faced with a situation such as they had never to meet before. In 1564 the allies besieged the Fort of Cannanore and destroyed the Portuguese ships in the harbour. A relief force was sent from Goa under Andre de Sousa, who was later on superseded by Goncalo Pereira Marmanaque. The troops in the fort were also reinforced, and both sides prepared to carry on the war with vigour.

The campaign started in earnest on the sea. The Malabar fleet of the Portuguese was divided into three squadrons. Maramanaque, with the larger portion of it, blockaded Cannanore and scoured the seas in front of Calicut. Dom Paulo de Lima Pereira was stationed to the north of it, while the general work of patrolling was done by a fleet of seven ships under Pedro da Silva. The last named commander fell in with a fleet of Calicut paraoes which he attacked. The paraoes were chased down the coast, but at Pudupattanam, a naval station of the Kunjali's, the Malabar fleet received reinforcements and turned on the enemy who fled after an indecisive conflict. Kunjali, the Calicut admiral, himself, was ready with a large and well equipped fleet. Venturing north he attacked Dom Paulo in the Bay of Bhatkal and gained a complete victory. Dom Paulo, who was on his way to Cannanore to help the beleagured garrison in that city, turned tail and returned to Goa, wounded in body and humiliated in spirit.

The continuous war in Malabar was seriously affecting the trade in pepper and other spices. Neither from Cannanore nor from Calicut was there anything to be had. Even in Cochin the trade was equally depressed owing to the hostility of the Rajah of Vadakkumkur and others. The Viceroy was, therefore, anxious to come to terms with Cannanore, where, though the siege had been raised after a stiff fight, the Portuguese position was by no means safe. The Rajah was, however, wearied of fighting and agreed to treat, and peace was again restored. This enabled the Portuguese to pursue the naval war with greater vigour. Alvaro Santomayor, with the fleet that was previously blockading Cannanore, turned his attention to Kunjali, whose campaign of guerilla warfare was doing great harm to Portuguese trade. So far it had been found impossible to chase him to his lair; and though Santomayor had as many as 20 ships under him, Kunjali still escaped his vigilance and continued his career of warfare. His depredations became so intolerable that the Viceroy, Dom Luiz de Atayde Conde de Atouqueria, despatched Martino Affonso de Miranda in 1569 with a large fleet of 36 vessels. This expedition met with no greater success. Kunjali eluded the vigilance of the Portuguese vessels, attacking them only under favourable conditions. Exasperated by these tactics, the Portuguese captain forced an engagement from a disadvantageous position; the battle ended in a victory for the Malabar fleet. De Miranda was wounded, and had to be carried to Cochin where he died. Another attempt to bring Kunjali to action was made the next year with no greater success. After these unsuccessful attempts, the Portuguese gave up, for the time, the idea of destroying Kunjali's power, and began a policy of attacking and destroying the coastal towns of Malabar. Dom Diogo de Meneses, who was in charge of the Malabar squadron, had under him in all about 40 vessels, and wherever he went he burnt, pillaged, and massacred without mercy. Among the ports which suffered from his devastating activities were Pandarini Kollam, Tirokode and Ponnani. Kunjali, on his side, carried the war into the enemy's own territory sailing as far north as Diu. His forces also gained a victory over some Portuguese ships commanded by Ruy Dias Cabral and Henrique de Meneses, 1569. In this battle the Portuguese lost 70 men including the captain Ruy Cabral, while his companion Dom Henrique de Meneses was taken captive.

Though the Zamorin expressed willingness to cease hostilities, the Portuguese would not agree, as they had made up their minds to take ample revenge for Kunjali's actions. But they had soon to repent of their mistake. At the failure of his overtures for peace, the Zamorin entered into an alliance with Adil Khan and "Nizamulcao" Murtaza Nizam ul Shah, the Mad. Adil marched on Goa, Nizam ul Khan on Chaul, and the Zamorin attacked the fortress of Chaliyam which was an eyesore to him. The Zamorin's fleet gained an initial victory. At the end of February 1570, he despatched a fleet under one of the Marakkars to help Nizamul Khan who was besieging Chaul. The fleet passed the Portuguese ships in the port and reached Chaul, but after a stay of twenty days the Marakkar returned without directly engaging the Portuguese ships. On his way back, the Calicut admiral made an unsuccessful attempt on Mangalore. He was soon overtaken and defeated off Cannanore by the squadron of Diogo de Meneses.

The Zamorin's attack by land on the fortress of Chaliyam was completely successful. The siege lasted for four months (June to September), when owing to the monsoon, the Portuguese ships were not in a position to bring reinforcements or otherwise render help. The Tofut ul Mujahideen gives a graphic description of the siege.[1] "Early in July the Zamorin sent a large force under one of his commanders to attack the Fort. The people of Tanur and Parappanangadi joined in large numbers and a great battle took place outside the walls in which the Portuguese suffered heavy defeat. They then returned to their citadel and took refuge in it. But the troops of the Zamorin surrounded it, and throwing up trenches around it, blockaded it with the greatest vigilance. In carrying on this siege the Zamorin expended vast sums of money. About two months after its commencement, he came down himself from Kunan to conduct the operations; and with such extreme vigour and activity did he pursue his measures, intercepting all supplies, that the stock of provisions of the Franks became entirely exhausted, and they were compelled to devour dogs and to feed on animals of a similar vile, impure nature. In consequence of this scarcity there came out of the fort every day large bodies of their servants, both male and female, who were not molested by the

1) Tofut· Page 166.

besiegers. Now although the Franks sent supplies to their countrymen shut up in Chaliyam from Cochin and from Cannanore, yet these never reached them, their convoys having been attacked and destroyed. During the blockade, the besieged sent messengers to the Zamorin offering to capitulate and deliver up to him certain large pieces of cannon which were in the fort and also to indemnify him for the expenses of war, besides some other concessions. But he refused to consent to these terms, although his ministers were satisfied with them. Shortly after when the Franks perceived their condition desperate from failure of their provisions and that they could make no easier terms, they sent messengers to the Zamorin, offering to deliver up the fort with its arsenal and all its cannon, provided a safe passage was afforded them and protection for their personal property guaranteed and he accepting these terms, the garrison marched out at midnight on the 10th of Jamadialakhur." The Zamorin demolished the fort "leaving not one stone upon another."

With their expulsion from Chaliyam, it may be said that the Portuguese effort to control Malabar came to an end. The war with the Zamorin, which began with the invasion of Calicut by Marechal Countinho, ended after 65 years of incessant struggle in the signal defeat of the Portuguese. They had hoped to put down the power of the Zamorin by a blockade of Calicut, but this after 12 years of trial had to be abandoned as a costly failure. They had hoped to break his power by building a fortress at Calicut and holding it as a pistol at his throat, a policy which had succeeded èminently at Cochin. This also ended in failure. The Zamorin agreed to the construction of a fort, but when the factor made an attempt to assert political authority the Calicut Ruler collected his forces and drove the Portuguese into the sea. The next attempt was to hold the strategic position at Chaliyam, and from there attack and harass the trade of Calicut. Great hopes were entertained of this scheme. When the fort was built the King of Cochin wrote jubilantly to the King of Portugal thus: "It seems to me that a great service was rendered to Your Highness by the Governor by building the fortress at Chaliyam because this tempers the Zamorin down so much that he will do what Your Highness may require of him."[1] This was in fact what the Portuguese had hoped for. But these dreams failed to materialise. For forty years the fight continued and it ended only with the withdrawal of the Portuguese from the mainland.

It is true that even after this the Portuguese continued to be in possession of Cochin for another 70 years. But their political power, so far as it ever existed, and the ambition to control Malabar and maintain effective authority over its rulers, ceased with this. They maintained a precarious foothold at Cannanore, Cochin, Cranganore, Procaud and Quilon; but in the territories over which the Zamorin ruled they had no factory or commercial house. Seventy years of conflict had come to nothing, and the victory in this prolonged struggle lay decisively with the Ruler of Calicut.

1) Letter dated 1533. Dec. 18. "Corpo Chronologico." Part 1. Maco 52 Document 23.

CHAPTER IX

THE FALL OF THE KUNJALIS

The continuous naval fight kept up by the Kunjalis on behalf of the Zamorin was extremely exasperating to the Portuguese. With the reconquest of Chaliyam, the power of Kunjali on the coast became practically irresistible. Kunjali III, who was the head of the family, had already won his laurels in many a fight, and now, since the Portuguese base on the Calicut coast was destroyed, it became possible for him to consolidate his power. From the grateful Zamorin whom he had served so well, he obtained permission to build fortresses and dockyards at Pudupattanam. Within two years after the Portuguese defeat at Chaliyam, Kunjali had built for himself the *Marakkar Kotta* and established himself there as a feudatory of the Zamorin. His power grew considerably and, on land, he exercised privileges and authorities enjoyed by Nair Chiefs.[1]

The Portuguese, though driven out from the mainland, did not give up the fight on the sea. A large naval force was despatched from Goa which harried and plundered the coastal towns. In 1572, a Portuguese force landed at Parappanangadi and pillaged the town and set fire to the mosques and temples. The main ports of the territory of Calicut, Trikodi,

1) "Vadakkan Pattu"—The Nair Ballads—mentions this.

Kapakad and Ponnani suffered heavily from these marauding expeditions. But even worse than this, the Portuguese ships began intercepting the rice trade with Tulunad, creating thereby a famine in the land. Zeinuddin mentions that in 1577 they captured 50 Arab vessels carrying rice, with the result that much distress was caused among the poor people. The town of Nileshwaram was attacked and reduced to ashes.

In 1578 the Portuguese Viceroy sent ambassadors to negotiate with Calicut. But the Zamorin was away then at a temple performing religious ceremony. The negotiations were, however, carried on by his ministers on his behalf. But they came to nothing, because the Portuguese demanded the right to build a fort at Funam. The Portuguese negotiators were, therefore, sent back; but the Zamorin, who did not want to renew hostilities, sent an embassy of his own to Goa which was received with great pomp and courtesy. The negotiations were reopened and, though they dragged on for some weeks, no agreement was reached.

Tired of useless diplomacy, the Portuguese again decided on war. In this course, they had the support of the King of Cochin, who was particularly anxious that the Portuguese and the Zamorin should not become friends. The Rajah of Cochin took the field with a large army, and a Portuguese contingent was sent to help him, while a naval attack, meant as a diversion, was made on the coast. The Zamorin's forces marched down south, and the Allies—the Cochinites and the Portuguese—attacked him with vigour, but were defeated.[1] "Exasperated by this defeat, the galliots of the Franks sailed out from Cochin" for the purpose of harassing the trade of the Zamorin. An attack was made on Chaliyam in the hope of recovering that strategic position, but it met with no success. The same tactics of chasing the ships and destroying the ports and villages on the sea coast, were continued by Mathias de Albuquerque. It did not seriously affect the Zamorin, especially as the fight on the sea did more harm to Portuguese trade than it did to him.

In the meantime there was trouble brewing in Cochin. The port dues of Cochin were shared between the Rajah and the Portuguese authorities. 9 per cent *ad valorem* duty was charged by the Portuguese and 3½ per cent by the Rajah. We have noticed how, under orders from the King, Dom Manuel, the Portuguese tried as early as 1530 to evade payment. As the Rajah protested vigorously the payments were renewed. In 1588, the Governor persuaded the ruler to give up that right. The people rose in revolt at this surrender of an important source of revenue. The captain of the fort appealed to Goa. The garrison in Cochin was reinforced, but the people refused to be cowed by this. The position was extremely grave, as an attack on Cochin by the local population openly in revolt against their own Rajah and against Portuguese Governor would mean immediate disaster. Realising the gravity of the situation the Portuguese authorities withdrew their claim.

---

1) "Tofut ul Mujahideen," p. 177.

One result of the agitation in Cochin was that negotiations were reopened with the Zamorin. The main object of the Portuguese was the erection of a fort at Ponnani which is an important centre for internal trade. Ruy Gonsalves de Camara, the uncle of the Governor, was sent on this mission, but the Zamorin was in no hurry. On one excuse or another, he refused to proceed with the negotiations for a considerable time, and agreed to the construction of a fort only with bad grace. Kunjali did not like this concession, especially as he felt that a Portuguese fort at Ponnani would be a constant menace to him. In 1586 he fought a battle with the Portuguese and defeated them. In 1589, Khwaji Musa, the nephew of Kunjali, fell in with a Portuguese squadron. Musa had with him more than twenty galleys. After a stiff fight the Portuguese ships were put to flight. These two victories gave the Kunjalis the command of the Malabar seas. Musa captured many Portuguese ships and caused much damage to their trade. For over two years Portuguese navigation was practically intercepted on the Malabar coast. Musa even contemplated attacking Colombo. A powerful fleet consisting of over 20 ships under Andre Furtado was sent by Mathias d'Albuquerque, the Viceroy, to destroy Musa's power. Musa was overtaken, and, in the battle that took place all his ships were destroyed, and he, himself, escaped with great difficulty by swimming to the shore. The destruction of Musa's fleet did not dishearten Kunjali. He took to the sea immediately with another fleet and swept the Portuguese ships off the Malabar coast. As his attacks were causing much damage, the Portuguese were willing to make peace, and, at the intercession of a Catholic priest, negotiations were opened which ended in a satisfactory settlement in 1591.

As usual peace did not last long, because the Zamorin would not accept the *cartas*, and the Portuguese insisted on treating all ships navigating without their authority as pirates. This action on their part led to reprisals on the part of the Zamorin, though the official attitude of peace was maintained on both sides. Kunjali was especially lucky. A richly laden galley returning from China was attacked and destroyed. To take revenge for this, a very powerful force was specially fitted up and sent down to the Malabar coast under Andre Furtado who had defeated Khwaja Musa in 1591. He captured 3 of the Zamorin's vessels with rich booty. The Malabar fleet which he attacked, though defeated in battle, escaped intact.

In 1595 Kunjali IV succeeded as Chieftain of *Marakkar Kotta* at Pudupattanam, and admiral of the Zamorin's fleet. He strengthened the fortifications, erecting towers heavily armed with cannon, and digging deep ditches. He was even more successful against the Portuguese than his father. But in his success he became proud and haughty and forgot his allegiance to the Zamorin. He cut off the tail of one of the Zamorin's elephants, and humiliated a Nair. The enraged Zamorin resolved to humble the pride of his overgrown subject and entered into an alliance with the Portuguese. The Viceroy sent Dom Alvaro de Abranches to negotiate the agreement. In the meantime

Mathias d'Albuquerque was recalled, and Francisco da Gama Conde de Vidiguera, a grandson of Vasco da Gama, was sent in his stead. As a result the agreement was delayed till 1597.

This agreement between the Zamorin and the Portuguese caused the Cochin Rajah great dissatisfaction. By various methods he tried to make the allies quarrel. He circulated the rumour that the Zamorin was actually in league with his rebellious officer, and that the agreement was only a ruse to get the Portuguese into his power. This rumour spread fast and made the Portuguese suspect the attitude of their ally. The Zamorin, however, advanced on Pudupattanam with a large army from the land side, while the Portuguese attacked it from the sea coast.

The *Marakkar Kotta* was at the mouth of the river, on a promontory, easily defensible and difficult of attack. It was strongly fortified and held by a trained and well armed garrison. The attack from the sea-side had also been foreseen, and Kunjali had gathered a powerful force to meet the naval attack of the Portuguese. The attack began by the Portuguese taking up a position at the mouth of the river from which they opened fire on the fort. The Zamorin's forces, which were attacking from the other side, were stiffened by a Portuguese contingent. With all these preparations, the first attack ended in disaster. Belcheor Ferreira's attack from the landside was easily repulsed. The attack of Luiz de Gama from the seaside also miscarried, resulting in heavy losses. The first effort, therefore, ended in failure as there was no co-ordination between the military and naval forces.

A new agreement was made in December 1599 with the Zamorin by Andre Furtado who was sent to take charge of the operations. The treaty provided that the princes of Tanur and Chaliyam were to be given as hostages and they were to remain in Cochin. In return the Portuguese were to give as hostages Dom Pedro de Noronha, Jeronymo Botelho, Antonio Matoso and two Fathers of the Society of Jesus. The Zamorin was to provide 1000 labourers, fifteen elephants and all the carpenters together with the wood necessary for the fight. The contingent that the Zamorin was to bring was to consist of 5000 Nayars, 2000 of whom were to be under the orders of the Portuguese commander. It was also agreed that if the fight was not over by the 20th of January, when the Zamorin would have to proceed to the Feast of Mamankam, the Rajah of Tanur was to be sent back. The Portuguese also agreed to give to the Zamorin half of the money, goods, artillery and ships captured.

Furtado, learning from the mistakes and defeat of his predecessor, proceeded with caution. First of all he cleared the river and erected batteries from which it would be possible to attack the enemy effectively. The attack was pressed with vigour. Kunjali, finding his position untenable, opened negotiations with the Zamorin requesting only that his men's lives should be spared. The Zamorin would not agree to this without consulting his ally, and Furtado was bent on destroying Kunjali's power. A new attack from both sides destroyed the Marakkar's power of resistance, and Kunjali surrendered on the condition that his life would be spared. He surrendered his sword to the Zamorin who yielded him to the Portuguese. Breaking their plighted word, the Portuguese put him to death at Goa.

Thus ended the power of the Kunjali Marakkars. It has been the custom of European writers, following Portuguese historians to call them "pirates". The Portuguese gave them this name, because it was their claim that they alone had the right to navigate the seas in virtue of the title that the King of Portugal took for himself. To them, any person who questioned their right on the sea was a pirate. Barroes, in fact, goes to the extent of saying that, though the right of navigating the seas belonged to all nations equally in Europe, in Asiatic countries it was the exclusive privilege of the Portuguese. Only on this basis could the Kunjalis be considered "Pirates." They were the admirals of the Zamorin. They held their land and authority from and under him. Even the title *Kunjali Marakkar* was his grant. They enjoyed a position and prestige equal to Nair Chieftains. They had to pay duties to the Zamorin[1] and take their orders from him, as the Portuguese found out. To call an opponent a pirate may be an easy way of discrediting him; but a family of hereditary naval commanders, who fought with success against the Portuguese for a century under orders from their King, could not be dismissed in that summary manner.

1) Pyrard I—338, 344.

We have no detailed information of the amount of losses which they were able to inflict. The Portuguese historians themselves agree that the activities of the Marakkars caused them incalculable harm. Every year they had to fit out new fleets to deal with the Marakkars' encroachments. Remy Defeynes de Monfot mentions that in one year the Malabar sailors captured 160 caravels from the Portuguese.[1] Finch says that in "one year the Malabars took six Portuguese vessels, captured one Ormuz ship and three frigates. Soon after they took 16 out of a fleet of 25 vessels from Cochin and had 50 frigates and galliots on cruise. They carry in each frigate 100 soldiers and in their galliots 200."[2]

Of their enterprise, energy and valour it is impossible to speak too highly. Though successive misfortunes overtook them, and the superior equipment of the Portuguese ships was sure to destroy them in open conflict every year, the Kunjalis fitted up new fleets. Time after time, their fleets were sunk and the crew mercilessly slain, but the varying fortunes of war did not deter them from further effort. Their flag flew from Colombo to Cutch. They knew no fear, and there is not a single instance of a Kunjali or his relation surrendering to the Feringhee. Even on the last occasion the Marakkar surrendered to his sovereign, whose authority he had defied, and not to the Portuguese Commander. Like true seamen, they took to the sea with its dangers and its fortunes. Their tactics

1) Somers—Collection of Travels.

2) Foster's Early Travels.

against the Portuguese, which were evolved after the retreat of the Egyptian forces in 1507, were to intercept trade, harass the enemy and avoid pitched battles. As a rule their vessels were faster, as Vasco da Gama discovered when he came out as Viceroy. Their armament, though less heavy than what the Portuguese ships carried, was effective and they used it with great skill.

It may be a matter of surprise that the Zamorin should have allied himself with the Portuguese to destroy the power of the Marakkars, who had served him so well for centuries, especially against the Portuguese during the previous one hundred years. The reasons are simple. The expulsion of the Portuguese from Chaliyam had removed the menace which had hung over his head like a sword of Damocles; and he was thereby relieved of the necessity of depending upon a strong naval force. Secondly, with the withdrawal of the Portuguese, Kunjali's power had increased and he began to claim for himself authority and position, which conflicted with the sovereignty of the Zamorin. In fact, he had become an overgrown subject. The fortresses and base he had constructed at Kottakkal gave him the belief that he was an independent Chieftain and no longer dependent on the Zamorin. Thirdly there was the growing antagonism of the Nair population, whose privileges and rights he ignored. Of this we have ample evidence in the popular ballads which are still extant.

The tombs of the Kunjalis can even now be seen at Kottakkal where the family still lives. They are held in great veneration by the Mahommedan population. There can be no doubt that the lives of these Chiefs reflect glory and honour on all Malabar; for their achievements against the naval tyranny of the Portuguese form indeed a great chapter in the history of Malabar.

CHAPTER X

THE LAST DAYS OF PORTUGUESE POWER

The destruction of the sea power of the Marakkars did not help the Portuguese in maintaining their supremacy unquestioned on the sea. A new and more dangerous rival had already entered the arena. In 1594, at a meeting of the leading merchants held at Amsterdam, it was decided to send a Dutch fleet to India. A company was formed, and a fleet of 4 vessels left for India the next year. Soon, other private companies followed. By 1599 the Dutch were firmly established in Eastern trade; and the English followed in their wake. The monopoly of India's trade with Europe, which the Portuguese had enjoyed for just a hundred years, ended with this. Even the trade slowly disappeared, while the forts and factories which they had established on the coast were gradually captured by the Dutch.

The nominal authority of the Portuguese in Malabar waters and their control of Malabar trade, through Cochin, Quilon and Cannanore continued for another half a century. But their political power in Malabar had vanished and the command of the sea was contested by the Dutch. Even the trade in pepper and spices, which had given them great profit in early days, languished. The continuous quarrels with the Chiefs and the hostility of the Syrian Christians whom the Portuguese had alienated by their religious persecution combined with the inveterate hatred of the Moors ruined their trade. Moreover, the traditional fight between the Zamorin and the Rajah of Cochin had broken out again, destroying the hopes of a revival in the trade with the Ruler of Calicut which the Portuguese had entertained.

While the fight against Kunjali was going on, the Cochin Rajah attacked Koratty Kaimal, one of the feudatories of the Zamorin, in the hope of embroiling Calicut with the Portuguese. As soon as the campaign against the Marakkar was over, the ruler of Calicut marched against his enemy, and, though the Cochin Rajah was driven out of the lands he had invaded, the Zamorin himself was wounded by a stray shot. A truce was arranged, but did not last long. The new Zamorin, who succeeded the destroyer of Kunjali, recognised that the invasion of Cochin could not succeed so long as the line of communication with that state was threatened by the fort of Cranganore. The Rajahs of Cranganore had been feudatories of the Zamorin from the earliest times. But, after the Portuguese had established themselves there, the Chief of Cranganore took advantage of the continued hostility between them and the Zamorin to declare his independence. With that extraordinary persistency which characterised the policy of the Rulers of Calicut, the Zamorin had never forgiven this defection. In 1536 he attacked and conquered Cranganore and re-established his own sovereignty. But the Chief, with the help of the Portuguese who had built a fort in his capital, again revolted. The establishment of the Portuguese at Chaliyam seriously prejudiced the Zamorin's claims against his feudatory and checked his activities in this quarter; but with its destruction the way was again open to him to attack Cranganore. When the new war with Cochin opened at the beginning of the century, the Zamorin called upon the Chief of Cranganore to help him with soldiers. As that Chief did not want to offend either the Portuguese who were helping the Rajah of Cochin, or the Zamorin who was his suzerain, he remained inactive. The result was that, as soon as the Ruler of Calicut was free, he attacked Cranganore and annexed its northern part to his own State. After this the Zamorin made preparations to attack the town and fortress of Cranganore, which were in the possession of the Portuguese. A contemporary description of the fortress of Cranganore is to be found in a Portuguese manuscript *Noticias da India*.[1] "Its fort," says the writer, "was built by Dom Miguel Bolin who defended it against many attacks from Calicut......The fortress is provided with a cathedral and an Archbishop appointed by the Holy See. The fortress has a captain for its maintenance with the garrison and artillery required for its defence, a misericordia and a hospital and a house of the Fathers of the Company of Jesus and another of St. Francis. The fortress is 100 fathoms in length from bastion to bastion and 8 in height

1) "Noticias da India"—India Office Manuscript. Portuguese translations Vol. I. Page 225.

and 6 spans in width. The settlement which is near the fortress contains a hundred married couples, forty Portuguese and the rest natives. The wall which surrounded the settlement is sixty fathoms and fifteen spans in height."[1]

The Zamorin decided to attack this fortress and was, in that effort helped by the Rajah of Parur, a Brahmin Chief who was ill disposed towards both the Portuguese and the King of Cochin. At this time, even the King of Cochin was not on friendly terms with the Portuguese though he did not dare to openly show his hostility. The Viceroy was, therefore, anxious not to embroil himself with the Zamorin, and sent an embassy to Calicut offering to open negotiations. The Zamorin knew that this was meant as a dilatory move, and, while accepting the large presents sent and receiving the embassy with courtesy, went forward with his preparations for the attack. Early next year he sent an army which surrounded the fortress and besieged it. The garrison was reduced to great straits. Enough provisions continued to reach Cranganore from Cochin, and the fort held out until the next year when relief arrived under Dom Barnardo de Noronha. The Dutch ships, which were hastening to the help of the Zamorin, were intercepted and the siege was raised.

But the minor Chiefs of Malabar had learned the lesson. They saw that a new force had entered the Arabian Sea, with whose help it would be possible for them to free themselves from the hated yoke of the Portuguese. The Dutch also realised that in Malabar

1) "Noticias da India"--Vol. I. Page 225.

the position of the Portuguese was precarious because of the hostility of the Princes; and for the next 30 years the attempt of the Dutch captains on the coast was mainly directed towards maintaining friendly relations with the Chiefs. This was in fact the end of the Portuguese power in Malabar. In the years that followed, they exercised little or no sway in the land as they had to fight both the English and the Dutch on the sea. In 1616 Captain Kealing, an English sailor, reached Cranganore; and the Zamorin agreed to sign a treaty with England by which he promised to give the English facilities for trade, if they, on their side, helped him to reconquer Cochin.[1] With the Dutch also the Zamorin had entered into negotiations about the reconquest of Cochin.

The Portuguese, on their side, were handicapped in this struggle for naval supremacy, by the indifference with which the Spanish Monarchy viewed Portuguese concerns in the East. Ever since Philip II had brought Portugal under his control, the interest which the Portuguese Kings had personally taken in the development of Eastern trade had vanished. Neither reinforcements nor instructions were received regularly from Portugal. Challenged on the sea both by the Dutch and the English, and hated by the Indian Powers, the Portuguese fought a losing battle and in spite of heavy odds maintained their position for a time. But, neither from the point of view of Malabar history, nor

1) Letters received by the East India Company from its servants. Vol. V. 1616.

from that of the history of India in general, is the struggle worth recording.

The opposition of even the minor Malabar Rulers increased when it became evident that the Portuguese power was weakening.

The condition of the Portuguese in India at this time was most deplorable. Public coffers were empty; the soldiers were not paid; and the rivalry between the religious Orders and the State hampered all effective action. The Jesuits and other religious bodies had become all-powerful. They took no notice of the orders of the Viceroy and usurped Royal jurisdiction and revenues. The Viceroy, writing in 1631 to the King, complained that in certain areas of Travancore, the Jesuits had become the real masters. The religious Orders were heavily subsidised from State revenues; and it is said that there were twice as many Portuguese priests as there were laymen of the same nationality in each city. As monks were given large allowances from the State, and as soldiers had often to go for months without pay, it became the common practice in the army to take holy Orders or go into a monastery. A great portion of the revenues of the State went for the upkeep of large bodies of priests.

A curious custom had also developed of sending out girls from the orphanage in Lisbon with dowries provided for in the orders of appointment for their husbands. One such girl brought with her an order for the Governorship of Cranganore. This scandal grew to such an extent that in 1627 an order was promulgated that all such dowry appointments should be limited to three years.

The decay of Portuguese power was most visible in the towns. The Conde de Vigueira, the Viceroy, wrote to the King in 1622, that Cochin which was the centre of spice trade had ceased to have any trade at all. Even before this time Cannanore had been neglected. Quilon also had become unimportant. These fortresses, the King was told by the Viceroy, were without guns or other effective means of defence. The revenue system was mainly based on duties and on the sale of cartazas. With the loss of trade the revenue from the first diminished. With the loss of power the revenue from the second ceased. The area of land that the Portuguese held was very small and was farmed out bringing in but little revenue. Thus it became impossible even to keep the fortresses in ordinary repair.

Even the Viceroyalty fell into disrepute. The Conde de Vigueira, when he was appointed Viceroy in 1521, wrote to the King reminding him that the appointment had been offered to three other people who had refused it, suggesting thereby that in going out to India as Viceroy he was doing a favour to his King. The home government also was negligent of what was going on in India; and, though successive Viceroys asked to be supplied with sufficient reinforcements, hardly any came from Portugal. In the meantime the power of the Dutch was greatly increasing.

Ever since the Dutch Company entered into the competition for Eastern trade, there was between them and the Portuguese unceasing and relentless war. The Portuguese continued to look upon the Dutch as intruders, and attempted to drive them out of the

Indian seas by force. This policy brought them into continuous conflicts, which swallowed up their revenue and ruined their trade. It is outside the purpose of this book to trace the fight between these two Powers. It is sufficient for our purpose to remember that, after consolidating their power in the Eastern Archipelago, the Dutch attacked the Portuguese in Ceylon in alliance with Rajah Simha. In 1638 three Dutch ships under Wilhelm Jacobs Coster made their first attack. After considerable fighting the Portuguese were expelled from the island in 1658. The Dutch established themselves in strength at Colombo, and turned their attention to the Portuguese establishments on the Malabar coast.

The first place to be attacked was Quilon. In December 1658 Ryklof Van Goens[1] captured that fort and, after establishing a strong garrison there, cruised the Malabar coast and returned to Colombo. The Portuguese, with the help of the Rani of Quilon, made a counter-attack, and the Dutch Governor withdrew the garrison to Colombo on the 14th of April 1659. The very next year Van der Meyden started again for the Malabar coast with a large force, reaching Azhikode, near Cranganore, on February 10, 1661. There the Dutch Governor entered into negotiations with the Zamorin, who had sent his heir-apparent as ambassador, and an agreement was reached,

1) Ryklof Van Goens was a man who had experience of Indian seas and of Indian conditions from his childhood. At the age of 10 he came out to the East with his father. Two years later he visited Coromandel Coast. When he was appointed to the Malabar expedition he was an Extraordinary Member of the Council at Batavia.

by which the contracting parties undertook to co-operate in order to drive out the Portuguese.

. The first attack of the Allies was on Pallipporto---Pallippuram. The importance of this fort lay in the fact that it provided an excellent base for attacking Cochin. After a determined resistance, the fort was stormed by the Dutch who handed it over, agreeable to their treaty, to the Zamorin. No effort was made immediately to attack Cochin. The Portuguese at once proceeded to strengthen their defences and to make preparations for withstanding a siege. The Dutch also kept this object in view, and entered into negotiations with the leading Chiefs on the coast.

The Kingdom of Cochin was then in a state of civil war. The cause of this lay in a series of conflicting adoptions which gave rise to rival claims to the throne.[1] It will be remembered that, early in the 16th century, the Portuguese under Albuquerque had interfered and dispossessed a senior branch of the family on the ground that the claimant belonging to that branch was a supporter of the Zamorin. The junior branch which was reigning became extinct in 1646, and adoptions were made both from the elder dispossessed branch and a collateral branch living at Palliviritti. Between these two branches, family feud broke out immediately, and, with the help of the Portuguese, the members adopted from the elder branch were again expelled. In 1650 the Gadi became vacant, and, without con-

1) There is an extremely interesting Malayalam book recently discovered and published by the government of Travancore which deals in detail with these adoptions and the wars that followed. "Padappattu"—vol. 5 of the Srimulam Library, published at Trivandrum.

sidering the claims of the elder branch, five princes from Tanur, who were traditional friends of the Portuguese, were adopted in 1658 and given the right to succeed.

The dispossessed princes of the elder branch appealed to the Zamorin who immediately took up their cause. With the intervention of the Zamorin, the nobles became divided into two parties, one supporting the Tanur adoptees, and the other the exiled princes. The leading supporters of the dispossessed princes were Adityavarman, Rajah of Vadakkumkur, and the Chief of Idappalli. The new adoptees found support in the Rajahs of Procaud and Valluvanad. The principals in the fight were, of course, the Zamorin, on behalf of the elder branch, and the Portuguese, on behalf of the new line.[1] The Nair Chief of Paliyam, who was the most powerful of the nobles of Cochin and the hereditary Prime Minister of the State, secretly supported the cause of the exiled princes. In 1661 ,when after the capture of Cranganore the Dutch admiral Van Goens was in Pallipuram, the Chief visited him and entered into a secret agreement. It was in the form of a request for protection which was granted by the pleasure of the Company. The following is the text of that agreement.

"I, Palietter Come Menone, Chief of the Island of Veipeen, being in difficulties on account of the Portuguese and other enemies named having done great harm to my land and my subjects, and caused trouble to me, for which reasons, finding myself powerless to resist such enemies, I am compelled to

1) "Padappattu", P. 14.

look out for a powerful nation which will maintain and protect my land and my subjects. With this object in view, I pray for and accept the protection of the Honourable Netherland East India Company in order that they may protect me against the enemies of my state. And at the same time I yield and surrender to the same Honourable Company my person, territory and subjects."[1]

This request was agreed to; and the Dutch, thereby, got their first foothold in Cochin. On the advice of the Paliyam Chief the claimant to the Cochin State, Vira Kerala Varma, who was in exile at Vadakkumkur, visited Colombo, and invited the Dutch Governor to help him to drive out the Portuguese. This was agreed to. We know the details of the proceedings in connection with this, not only from Portuguese and Dutch sources but also from a contemporary Malayalam Chronicle, the "Padappattu" already referred to. The plan, agreed to, was that the Zamorin should invade Cochin from the North, and Vira Kerala Varma, with the help of his allies, the Vadakkumkur and Thekkumkur Rajahs, should attack Cochin from the South, while the admiral was to attack it from the sea.

In the autumn of 1661 the Supreme Government at Batavia fitted out another expedition, with Jacob Hustart, Councillor, as Civil Chief and Admiral Van Goens as Commander. Captain Nieuhoff, the explorer and writer, was on one of the ships. The fleet took a heavy train of artillery from Colombo on the 7th of

1) Selections from the records of the Madras Government (Madras 1911). No. 13, p. 124.

October, and sailed for the Malabar coast. Meeting the ships of Commodore Roodhas at Manapare on the 15th of November, the expedition arrived before Quilon on the 7th of December. Immediately, a powerful body of soldiers was landed, and on the 8th they marched "in battle array into the country."[1] The Portuguese in Quilon offered no resistance. The only opposition, that the party met with, came from the Nairs of the Queen of Quilon, who had built a redoubt from which they fired on the Dutch. Though the firing did very little actual harm, it kept the Dutch near the shore, and prevented them from advancing. The Dutch commander, therefore, decided to cut down the forest on the side and take the artillery behind the redoubt. "Immediately all our carpenters were set to work to cut down bushes and trees while the seamen were employed in levelling the grounds to make way for the Artillery." The Nair army holding the redoubt withdrew. The fort was captured. "We continued our march," says Nieuhoff, "to the city of Koling, passing all the way a great many fine plantations, surrounded on all sides with walls, the road betwixt them being very narrow."[2] The next day, on the 10th, the main attack on the city began. Goskeled commanded the van, Roodhas the rear, and Ryklof Van Goens directed the operations. The enemy fought bravely, but were defeated. The Dutch captured the town and immediately set fire to the palace and the temple attached to it.

---

1) "Nieuhoff's Voyages". Churchill's collection of Voyages. Vol. II, p. 215.
2) Ibid.

After capturing Quilon, Van Goens, with 30 ships, appeared before Cochin on the 1st of January 1662. Landing his troops at Ayacotta he proceeded to lay siege to the fort of Cranganore, which was defended by Urband Fereira. Preparations were made for a regular siege and all the necessary material was landed from the ships. Though considerable resistance was offered and the defence conducted with skill, the Dutch were able to storm the fort, because the Chief of Paliyam, who had already entered into a treaty with the Dutch, betrayed to the Admiral the plans of the Portuguese. Then the Dutch forces moved south, and made preparations for an immediate attack on Cochin. At Vaipin, which was an island belonging to the Paliyam Chief, they established their headquarters in a Roman Catholic Church, and erected temporary defence works. From these an attack was first made on the Cochin palace which was completely successful. Adrian Van Rheede,[1] an ensign, burst into the palace and took possession of the person of Rani Gangadhara Lakshmi, the puppet set up by the Portuguese on the Cochin throne. Three out of the five Tanur princes died in the fight. The Rani, herself, was handed over to the Zamorin as prisoner.

The next attempt was to cross the back-waters and establish the Rajah on the mainland. Before it could be done, the Rajah of Procaud, whose power had greatly increased during the last half century, arrived

1) Adrian Van Rheede came of a noble family. Later, he became Baron Van Hydrecht. He deserves to be remembered for the monumental work on Indian Botany.—The Horticus Malabaricus—which he was instrumental in producing.

in support of the Tanur princes and held the shore. Foiled in this attempt the Dutch and their allies turned to the fortress of Cochin. An attempt was made to blockade it from all sides. When the position was desperate the Viceroy at Goa was moved to decisive action and despatched a fleet of five ships. The Rajah of Procaud also came up with reinforcements. The siege was raised, and the Dutch withdrew temporarily.

The Dutch returned with greater forces as soon as the monsoon was over. With the help of the Paliyam Chief and the Prince of the dispossessed branch, the Dutch established a blockade. Help came to the Portuguese from the side of the Rajah of Procaud, but after a heavy engagement the Nair contingent of that ruler was defeated. After two months, spent in artillery bombardment and preliminary skirmishes, an assult was decided upon. For 8 days and nights the attack continued unabated. Desertions thinned the ranks of the Portuguese and a close blockade was maintained from the side of the sea. In this hour of peril, the Portuguese inside the fort acted with great heroism. Though reduced to extremity, and with no hopes of relief from Goa, they held on to the very last. But their position was hopeless. A final attack made simultaneously on three points, though resisted with vigour by the Portuguese, ended in success. The Portuguese commander surrendered. Arrayed in black and solemn mourning clothes, and followed by his Captains, the Portuguese, commander, who had fought hard and revived even in defeat the memories of Pacheco and Albuquerque, marched up to the Dutch Admiral and handed over the keys of the town to him. With this act of surrender the Portuguese flag ceased to fly over Malabar. Cranganore was handed over to the Zamorin in accordance with the treaty. Over the fortresses at Cochin, Cannanore and Quilon the flag of the Portuguese had given place to the flag of Holland. The ruins of a fine fortress, a small population of topasses and a Bishopric at Cochin are all that is left of the glory of Vasco da Gama and Albuquerque. It vanished as suddenly as it arrived, leaving behind nothing but the family names of a few Eurasians to remind one of the days when the Portuguese held the mastery of Indian trade and to keep alive that memory.

CHAPTER XI

PORTUGUESE POLICY IN MALABAR

It is customary to speak about the "Portuguese Empire" or "Portuguese Power" in India as if it were something distantly alike, and predecessor to, the British Empire. This feeling is reflected in the writings of most European writers. The Portuguese, themselves, held that they were the Lords of India; and, following them, European writers have, almost without exception, echoed this view. One writer in the Journal of the Asiatic Society even works out a parallel between British power and the "Empire" of the Portuguese in India.[1] But all such views are coloured by the conception of the present state of British Power and do not in any sense agree with historical facts. The Portuguese never had any "Empire" in India. They had a few coastal towns, and their authority never extended beyond a few miles of their naval bases. The only territorial possession of any considerable extent over which they ruled was Goa—and Goa was an easily defensible island.

As against the rest of the European Powers they had a monopoly of Indian trade for about a century; of this we shall speak later. But even this monopoly of trade, based as it was on naval supremacy, was never accepted by Indian Powers. The sea power of the Zamorin was

---

1) Reade J. R. A. S. 1898 P. 589.

not effectively broken, as the preceding pages have shown, till the capture of Kunjali's fort in 1599. By that time the Dutch had already entered the arena and had become a serious rival on the sea. Thus, in no sense is there any justification for the facile statements commonly made about a "Portuguese Empire" in India or even an effective Portuguese Power as a factor in Indian politics.

So far as Malabar was concerned this was undoubtedly the case. The hundred years' war with the Zamorin, which was essentially a bid for land power, failed miserably with the capture, by that ruler, of the fortress at Chaliyam. The Portuguese commercial monopoly and political authority did not affect the area between Cannanore and Cranganore, and nowhere did it extend beyond the ports in which they had built fortresses of their own. Such fortresses existed at Cannanore in the land of the Kolathiri Rajah of Chirakkal, at Cranganore, at Cochin, at Procaud and at Quilon. In these places, and especially at Cochin, something like political suzerainty was developed, but its extent was limited by the fact that the power of the Rajahs concerned did not extend beyond a few miles of territory.

Of all the rulers in alliance with the Portuguese, the most considerable, from the point of view of royal power as well as of wealth, was the Kolathiri Rajah of Chirakkal. Though during the first few years the relations between him and the new comers were extremely cordial, the Portuguese, by their high-handedness in disregarding their own safe-conduct given to one of the ships belonging to Mammali Marakkar, made him an enemy. In the time of Albuquerque the Rajah was forced to dismiss his Minister and yield to the wishes of the Portuguese Commander. But, as we have seen, his relations with the Commander never again became cordial. In the time of Martim Affonso de Sousa hostilities broke out between the Rajah and the Portuguese as a result of the murder, by the Governor's agent, of Bakr Ali, another relative of Mammali. A bitter war which lasted for many years was the result of Payo de Noronhas' rudeness to the Kolathiri in 1558, and peace had to be purchased after the Cannanore garrison had undergone great privations. In fact, so far as the Rajah of Cannanore was concerned, he maintained his independent position and resisted with success the attempts of the Portuguese to intervene in his internal affairs. In this he was successful mainly because of the fact that, though his territory extended up to the coast, his own capital was at Chirakkal, a few miles inland, away from the reach of the guns from Portuguese ships. Thus at Cannanore, though there was a fort with considerable garrison, the Portuguese never had any political power and, whenever an attempt was made, the fortress itself was besieged and the trade of the factory put a stop to.

At Cochin and at Quilon, this was not the case. In both these places the Portuguese exercised effective political supremacy. The position of the Cochin Rajah, especially, was that of a vassal maintained on the throne by the favour of Portugal. The crown which the Rajah wore was made in, and sent from, Portugal. From the earliest times the Portuguese made it clear that the Rajah of Cochin stood to them in a position different from other Malabar princes. Even in the time of Almeida in 1505 they had interfered to set aside dynastic custom and to secure the succession of one favourable to themselves. At that time also the Cochin Rajah took an oath of allegiance to the King of Portugal. In all Portuguese correspondence the Rajah of Cochin was called on as a faithful "servant" to help both by men and by money. On the least provocation, the Portuguese did not hesitate to imprison him and to treat him with extreme incivility. Thus in 1510, Nuno Caliste Brocco, who was captain of the Cochin Fort, interned the Rajah in his palace as he was afraid that the Rajah might abdicate. He even refused the Rajah permission to retire and do religious work as was the unbroken custom of the head of the Cochin family. Albuquerque in fact openly told the Rajah that it was the will of Portugal, and not the custom of the State, that was binding on Cochin. During the century and a half that Portuguese captains exercised their authority in the fortress of Cochin, the Rajahs of that territory were virtually prisoners. Even the taxes, which by treaty should go to the Rajah, were not given to him. His temples were desecrated in spite of piteous appeals, and his own person was often insulted and outraged. In the family quarrels of Cochin the Portuguese regularly intervened. In every way the Rajah of Cochin was in a much worse position than when he was under the Zamorin.

The reason of this was that the Rajah of Cochin had no territorial possessions except in the immediate neighbourhood of the fortress. The land, on the other shore of the backwater, was held by the Anchi Kaimals, who were powerful Nair barons who owned but nominal allegiance to the Rajah. There was no territory on the mainland which accepted the Rajah's direct authority. The Chiefs and barons sympathised with the Zamorin and were in constant revolt. The Rajah, himself, was living practically a prisoner, within a furlong of the Portuguese fort. Thus the control of the Cochin Rajah gave them no political authority, but was helpful only in so far as they were able to press forward their schemes under cover of the Rajah's prestige and authority.

The Rajahs of Procaud and Quilon were also subordinate allies. By the first treaty that Lopo Soares made with the Queen of Quilon, that State received a share of the customs, but the Portuguese, when they acquired greater power, refused to abide by this clause. The Rajahs of Procaud were brought under the influence of Portugal only in 1580. Their position never became so bad as that of either the Rajah of Cochin, whose nominal vassal he was, or that of the Queen of Quilon. He advanced greatly in the favour of the Portuguese, who gave him the title of "*brother in arms*" to the King of Portugal. The only other ruler, with whom the Portuguese were on friendly political relations was the Rajah of Tanur—the ruler of Vettathu Nad. From this Chief they obtained the island of Chaliyam. The Rajah of Tanur was greatly supported by the Portuguese, who endeavoured to make him a Christian. One of the Rajahs, as mentioned previously, visited Goa and was received into the Church, but when the Zamorin's call came he abandoned the foreigner and marched at the head of his army to Vaduthalai.

Thus, except in the towns of Cochin, Procaud and Quilon, the Portuguese had no effective political authority of any kind. But they maintained a close and friendly political relationship with the minor Chieftains in the interior, without whose friendship they could not procure the cargo of spices which was their main concern. Their friendship was secured by a yearly subsidy in gold. The Rajahs of Vadakkumkur, Procaud, Udaimperur, Parur and Mangat received 1800 fanams each. This subsidy kept the Rajahs in good humour, increased their sense of importance, and secured their friendship. In the time of Martim Affonso de Sousa these payments were discontinued, and this action contributed materially to the success of the Zamorin in the subsequent wars against the Portuguese. This act of Martim de Sousa, which alienated the minor Chiefs, was not so much due to any meanness on the part of that Governor as to a change of policy. From the time of Albuquerque there have been two schools of opinion on the question of Indian policy. Albuquerque held that a firm military power, based on fortresses which can be defended by the guns of ships, was necessary if the trade with India was to be successfully carried on. He had no idea whatever of any territorial empire but he recognised—as his letters make clear—that, without a military power based on fortresses, trade with India was not secure. As a further development of this idea, he carried out a policy of alliances with minor Chiefs, on a footing of equality with the powerful ones like the Zamorin, and on a footing of supremacy with minor Rajahs like the Chief of Cochin. But this policy had its opponents. In fact Dom Francisco d'Almeida had himself expressly denounced it as leading to political weakness. "With respect to our fortress in Quilon," he said, "the greater the number of the fortresses you hold, the weaker will be your power. Let all our forces be on the sea, because if we should not be powerful at sea, everything will be at once against us."[1] After the time of Albuquerque the tendency was more and more to emphasise this point of view. Wherever the Portuguese had a direct and definite hold on the ruler, as at Cochin and Quilon, they put forward increasing claims and asserted their direct authority. But the policy of political control over the Chiefs in the interior was given up.

The main Portuguese fortresses in the Malabar coast were built with a double purpose, to overawe the local ruler and to control the export of pepper. In Cochin, the Rajah's palace being only a few yards away from the fortress, the political object was completely successful. In Cannanore and Quilon also it met with partial success. The commercial purpose was made clear from the very beginning. Almeida advised King Manuel to have a "strong castle in Cranganore on a passage of the river which runs to Calicut, because it would hinder the transport that way of

1) "Annaes das Sciencias e Letteras"—April 1858 (Lisboa).

a single speck of pepper."[1] The fortress at Chaliyam was built expressly for the purpose of controlling the trade in the Zamorin's territory, as that island, by its position on the Beypore River, commanded the natural waterway in the southern portion of the Kingdom of Calicut. When the Zamorin expelled the Portuguese from that fort the prospects of trade in that area vanished with it.

Each fortress was practically a Portuguese settlement. Within the area surrounded by the walls only Portuguese and Latin Christians were allowed to stay. The native inhabitants, unless they became Christians and gave the women in irregular marriage to Portuguese soldiers, were expelled from within the fortress. Each fortress was thus a small Portuguese colony. According to the *Noticias da India*,[2] even in Cranganore there were living in 1600 a hundred married couples, of whom 40 were Portuguese and the rest converted Christians. Cochin, of course, was different. It was governed as a city—that is, had municipal and other rights, with officers of justice and revenue, a misericordia and a hospital, besides numerous ecclesiastical and religious establishments. Its captain and garrison were paid out of the revenues of the land.

This arrangement, by which the Portuguese and their dependents were segregated in small areas, made a division of justice easy. The general arrangement about justice was as follows: "when any Nair or native of the land or Moor had any strife or contention, the

1) "Annæs das Sciencias e Letteras"— April 1858 (Lisboa).
2) P. 225.

Nair or native shall be tried by the local ruler, while Portuguese subjects were sent before the captain of the fortress." This privilege of the Portuguese was gradually extended to native Christians in the country of the smaller Rajahs. In the treaty with Quilon in 1544 it was laid down that Christians, when they were guilty of crime, should be sent for punishment to the Portuguese captain. Portuguese justice whether applied to themselves or to the Indian Christians, was of the most barbarous kind. In 1524 Vasco da Gama, himself, had 3 Portuguese women publicly whipped for the very inadequate reason of having come out on shore against his orders. Punishments for ordinary people were cruel and inhuman: but, so far as the nobility was concerned their privileges were kept intact. No fidalgo could be punished in India.

It is a matter of importance to note that this division of justice and the rigid exclusion of non-Christians from within the fortresses helped the Portuguese to exercise their authority without coming into conflict with the local rulers. If they had attempted to administer law to the native population with whom they came into contact, it must have immediately led to friction. But in this matter the Portuguese were wise; and even their Inquisition had authority only over Indian Christians living within the fort and near enough to be under actual control.

In relation to other states and rulers the Portuguese recognised no principle save that of strength. As Barroes declares, "The Moors and Gentiles are outside the law of Jesus Christ—which is the law that everyone must keep under pain of damnation and eternal fire. If then the soul be so condemned what right has the body to the privileges of our laws? It is true that they are reasoning beings and might, if they lived, be converted to the Faith, but in as much as they have not shown any desire as yet to accept this, we Christians have no duties to them."[1] It is on this simple principle that Portuguese policy towards Indian states was based. The result was that, except in Cochin and Quilon, where the Chiefs became absolute vassals, the Indian rulers strongly resisted their encroachments and were always in open fight against their pretensions. Never were they able to gain either the confidence or the respect of the people with whom they came in contact. The popular idea, which was on the whole right, was that the Portuguese were, as a nation, treacherous, untrustworthy and barbarously cruel. The cruelties of the early adventurers, especially of da Gama, were never forgotten. The action of Goncalo Vaz, who disregarded an official safe-conduct and captured Mammali Marakkar's boat killing all the crew and sewing them up in sails, is but a single example of the kind of atrocities which have disgraced the Portuguese name in India. *Kerala Pazhama*, a native Chronicle of the 17th century, gives a graphic description[2] which reminds one irresistibly of the Anglo-Saxon Chronicles which describe the devastations of Robert of Belleme, Geoffrey de Mandeville, and the robber barons. Nor were their exploits of this nature confined

1) Barroes 1. 6. 1.
2) "*Kerala Pazhama*" Page 104.

to the sea. Whenever there was an opportunity for plunder, they never allowed either considerations of humanity, religion or good faith to stand in their way. The plunder of the Tevalakkara temple has already been alluded to. Another example, which is particularly interesting, will show the standard of honour that obtained generally among the Portuguese in India. At Pallurithi, near Cochin, there was a temple which was held specially sacred by the Rajahs of Cochin. This temple was credited by rumour to possess untold wealth. The Rajah of Cochin was the closest ally and friend of the Portuguese on the West Coast and knowing that the Governor was thinking of organising an expedition to plunder it, he expostulated with him and got his word of honour that no such attempt would be made. But the Governor, though himself desisting from it, authorised his subordinate to attack the temple, and an expedition organised under his own personal care left for Pallurithi. It was unsuccessful in its immediate object. This incident, especially as it is but one of many similar acts by the Portuguese, may be taken as showing the general unscrupulousness of the Portuguese in India.

How far they set honour and scruple at naught, can be seen from the practice followed by one of the captains in issuing safe-conducts which consisted of words to the following effect:—[1] "The owner of this ship is a very wicked Moor. I desire that the first Portuguese captain to whom this may be shown may make a prize of her." The treachery of Bastiao de

1) Rowlandson "Tofut ul Mujahideen" (see note on p. 90).

Sousa in murdering Bakr Ali at the Cannanore beach, where they had met for negotiations, was the cause of a bitter war. The history of the Portuguese in India is full of incidents of this kind. Albuquerque, himself, was not much better in this respect, as he confesses to have persistently requested the heir apparent of the Zamorin to poison that King.

Devastation of land and property was systematically followed in the campaign of coastal raids by which the Portuguese attempted to revenge the defeats inflicted by the Kunjalis. At Cannanore alone, on one occasion in 1564, the Portuguese soldiers felled 40,000 palm trees.

Of the organisation of Portuguese government in India much need not be said. In their Malabar settlements, the political organisation was, even for that age, surprisingly ineffective. There was no territory to be governed in Malabar; and hence the only system they developed was a peculiar combination suited for purposes of trade and military defence. The towns were under the command of a captain---that of Cochin being appointed direct from Portugal. He worked under the orders of the Governor who, after Albuquerque's time, resided at Goa and was responsible for the defence and ordinary administration of the fort. In Cochin, as we have already pointed out, there was an officer of Justice and of Revenue. The major part of the customs of the port of Cochin belonged to Portugal, and its collection and administration were the duty of the Controller of Revenues, who was also appointed from Portugal. This position was held for some time by that remarkable man, one of the few honest

Portuguese officials who came out to India, Affonso Mexia who did a great deal to put the finances of that town in order. This office of the Treasurer of Cochin was later on found to be of little use, as the Malabar trade began to languish as a result of the hostility of the local Chiefs. Cosme Annes, writing to the King in 1549, declared that, "the office of the treasurer of Cochin is of no further use than an unavoidable expense, causing further damage to the exchequer of Your Highness."[1] It is characteristic of the Portuguese that, till 1510, there was no auditor at all at the factory. Affonso Albuquerque protested strongly against this state of affairs and wrote to the King: "It appears to me, Senhor, that it is not right to have such a standing as you have at Cochin without an auditor for house and factory. Your business has so increased that it cannot be trusted to men who say 'I will render an account when I go to Portugal' and meanwhile would have in their possession two or three thousand cruzados or even more."[2] As long as the great Governor was in India he was able to enforce discipline in financial as well as in ordinary political administration; but his fight—not wholly successful—with Antonio Reall and the rest of the corrupt gang which controlled Cochin trade, showed that even under his rigorous rule the Portuguese administrative system was corrupt and inefficient.

This obvious inefficiency in the organisation of government was emphasised by two factors which seem most strange to modern eyes. One was the right which

1) "Corpo Chronologico." Part I. Maco 83. Document 60.
2) "Cartas", Letter dated 16th October 1510.

subordinate officials had of corresponding direct with the King and high officials in Portugal. Every mail took to Lisbon slanderous letters from almost every official of importance in India in which accusations were freely made against superior officers leading often to sudden changes of policy and much scandal. Albuquerque was so disgusted with this that he wrote to the King about Antonio Reall, his subordinate in Cochin, "You recommend Antonio Reall to me—considering how he has abused me calling me, thief, Moor, coward and the confidence you place in him, it is I who want a recommendation to him". "What reigns here," he says in another letter, "is the wish to acquire authority before Your Highness by representing to you the defects of others."[1] In a letter written by one of the subordinate officials to the King appears the following passage about the Governor: "I make known to Your Highness that Lopo Soares came to India in an evil hour."[2] This system of private correspondence by officials continued to the end, and much of the trouble between the officials in India was due to it.

More than even this, there was no sense of loyalty among the officials even as against the enemies. The officers at Cochin were always intriguing with the local Chiefs. Not a few of them were said to be in league with the enemies of Portugal. Gaspar Gonsalves openly tells the King that his "esteemed fidalgo of the Household, Antonio Reall of Cochin was leagued with the robbers."[3]

1) "Cartas" 1st April 1512.
2) "Gavitas Antigas" Maco 6 Document No. 51. 3) Ibid.

Lorenco Moreno, another officer at Cochin, got an officer of the Rajah of Cochin to write to the King of Portugal praising his qualities and recommending him for promotion. Naturally discipline was most lax; and as fidalgos could not be punished in India there was almost complete disorganisation when the Governor was a weak or timid man. Even in the time of Albuquerque personal quarrels played a great part in Portuguese history as the struggle between d'Almeida and him proves. Desertion to the enemy was a common affair, and fidalgos of note, not infrequently, took service with Indian rulers after committing some crime for which they would have been punished if they had returned to Lisbon. The case of Goncalo Vaz Coutinho is of particular interest as it sheds much light on the discipline of Portuguese officers. Coutiñho belonged to a well-known and powerful family in Portugal. In India his life was a career of crime for which the Governor imprisoned him along with some others. Coutinho bribed one of the officials and walked out of prison in daylight with his other friends and straight away joined the army of Adil Shah who was fighting against Portugal.

When discipline was so lack, and officials were fighting against each other, it was clearly impossible to build up an administrative system. Even if some Governor like Albuquerque or Joao de Castro wanted to improve discipline and bring into existence an efficient system of government, the right of private trade and the great privileges of the Church would have made reform impossible. These two may be said to be the distinguishing characteristics of the Portuguese system. The permission to engage in private trade was given to all officers, and the result, as we have pointed out earlier, was that each man engaged only on his business, leaving the King's affairs to look after themselves. Even the soldiers were allowed to trade after serving 9 years, without which inducement few men would have come out on service. The effect of this was disastrous. The perquisites of office were in fact the only consideration which made officers accept appointments. The Governorship "of India" was the easiest way to mend a ruined fortune, and, with one or two exceptions, most of the Governors who came out to India amassed enormous wealth by every possible means.

The vested interests of the Church were even more powerful than those of the officials. Of this we shall speak later on.

It should be clear from what has been said that nothing in the nature of a financial or administrative system was developed by the Portuguese. In fact, compared to that of the Portuguese, the Government of the Zamorin or of Adil Shah was better organised and more efficient. But we should not forget that Europe, at the end of the 15th century and during the course of the 16th, was only slowly evolving out of the feudal system. Organised Government, such as we know it now, existed nowhere in Europe. The indiscipline of the Portuguese officers was but a faint echo of the rebellious attitude of the baronage in Europe. There was no such thing as national patriotism in the 15th century when

Frenchmen were fighting in alliance with the English against their King, and Englishmen claimed to be French rather than English. The Portuguese were thus, in no way different from other European nations. The only difference was that at the time that other European peoples developed their political systems and organised their national life, Portugal had the misfortune to fall under the yoke of foreigners.

But on one thing Portuguese policy was definite from the very beginning. "Let it be known for certain," wrote d'Almeida, the first Viceroy, "that as long as you may be powerful at sea you will hold India as yours, and if you do not possess this power, little will avail you a fortress on shore."[1] From this policy the Portuguese never departed. To maintain the command of the sea, the Portuguese captains were prepared to take the most heroic measures. Their imperialism, if we may use a modern term, was a system of naval bases extending from Ormuz to Malacca from which they could command all trade, and hold to ransom the vessels of other nations. They realised that once the command of the high seas was lost to them, they could not possess the trade of India. The system of blockades by which they tried to ruin the trade of Indian States was not wholly successful, especially in Malabar, but they were able to command the main line of communication between Arabia, Egypt and India. Their important naval station in Malabar was Cochin where they had a well furnished

1) Annals of Sciences and Letters. April 1658.

magazine and the necessary equipments for the repair of ships.

One point with regard to Portuguese military policy is worthy of notice. At least from the time of Albuquerque the Portuguese decided to use Malabar men under the control of Portuguese officers in their fights with Mahommedan rulers. This policy, which was perfected later under Dupleix and Clive, came to be the basis of European rule in India. But the credit of the discovery must go to the Portuguese who used Malabar troops extensively in their campaigns. Many Malabarese even attained distinction in the service of Portugal. One individual who deserves special mention is Antonio Fernandes Chale, a Nair convert, who held various commands and was created a Knight of the Order of Christ. He died fighting at the battle of the river Sanguiler in 1571 and was buried with high honours in Goa.

The Portuguese authority was not based on any great military strength. There was only sufficient garrison in each fort to defend the place; and when it came to offensive actions the Portuguese met with but little success even as against minor Chieftains. Albuquerque, who was the only Governor who pleaded for a definite military policy based on fortresses, wanted no more than 3,000 soldiers to garrison and protect the factories. He wrote to the King in a letter dated 1st April, 1512, "Furthermore do I say Senhor that for effecting treaties with India and for the establishment of factories, such as are necessary for your service.......for three years would I keep three thousand men here, well armed and with every equipment for erecting fortresses." As long as Albuquerque was in command he kept up an efficient force and strained every nerve to do so. His successor, Lopo Soares, neglected the army; and thereafter the Portuguese military power was never a menace to any Indian Ruler. The soldiers who were sent out from Portugal were a disorderly rabble who had neither discipline nor military experience. Their pay was always in arrears, and it is on record that the company that came out in 1548 had to beg in the streets for food. No soldier was entitled to receive his pay until after one year's service in India, and even then payment could only be made after unnecessary and prolonged formalities.

The Portuguese policy towards the Indian communities in Malabar is of interest. Their religious policy has to be reserved for later discussion. From the social and political point of view it may be noted that converts to Christianity enjoyed all the privileges of the Portuguese citizens, and no distinction based on colour or race was recognised. The main and central fact of their relations with Indian communities was the encouragement of inter-marriage. The Portuguese had no kind of racial prejudice, and from the very beginning their relations were socially cordial. Albuquerque started a policy of encouraging inter-marriage, presiding at the functions himself and giving dowries to couples so married. Lands and houses were allotted to them within the fortress walls. They were exempted from paying customs especially for silk from China and for sugar from Portugal. Even for the rest they paid only four per cent. to the Rajah of Cochin. "I was in Cochin," wrote Cæsar Frederick, the Venetian traveller, "when the Viceroy of the King of Portugal wrought what he could to break the privilege of the citizens and to make them pay customs as others did; at which time the citizens were glad to weigh their pepper in the night that they landed the ships with all that went to Portugal and stole the custom in the night. The King of Cochin having understanding of this would not suffer any more pepper to be weighed. Then presently after this, the merchants were licensed to do as they did before and there was no more speech of this matter, nor any wrong done."[1] The rights of married men were indeed very considerable. It should be remembered that the Portuguese, themselves, brought no women with them to India. The difficulties of the voyage and the precariousness of life in India made settled family life among Europeans impossible. The idea of regular marital connections "by the regulations of Albuquerque" became, therefore, the custom, and helped much to keep the Portuguese flag flying in their fortresses even when their military strength had become negligible.

Towards the Mahommedans the attitude of the Portuguese was one of inveterate hostility. Their one idea was to root out the trade of the Moors and to destroy the Mahommedans as a race so far as possible. This was not only due to commercial rivalry, but to a hostility which the Iberian Powers had inherited from their

1) "Hakluyt's Voyages" Vol. V. pp. 392-395.

long-drawn out fight with the Moors in Spain and Africa. Whenever a Moor was captured the most barbarous tortures were inflicted on him and he was either killed or made a slave. The whole history of the Portuguese in India is nothing but a commentary on the statement of Barroes that the Moors were the "Enemies of God". Towards the Hindus they had no such enmity. Their relations with Hindu noblemen and Rajahs in Malabar were very cordial from a social point of view. When friendly relations existed between the Zamorin and the Portuguese, the scruples and superstitions of the Hindu ruler were respected by the Portuguese. To the Nairs as a whole they behaved with great consideration. The policy of religious persecution against the Hindus, which was attempted in Goa, was never tried in Malabar. The relations between the Native Christians and the Portuguese were of a most complicated nature and deserve to be treated specially.

CHAPTER XII

PORTUGUESE RELIGIOUS POLICY IN MALABAR

The Portuguese, we are told, came to India with a Cross in the one hand and a sword in the other. Their own pretensions in the East were based first on the Bull of Nicholas V, dated January 8th 1454, by which Affonso V was given, by virtue of the pontifical and apostolic authority of the Pope, exclusive right to all the countries that might be discovered by the Portuguese in Africa and India. The conversion of the inhabitants of the lands so discovered was to be one of the objects of Portuguese policy. In fact Dom Joao II, who was the real originator of the expedition, had much of this evangelistic spirit in him. To the pious Kings of mediæval Europe conversion of the heathens seemed to be an imperative duty.

Neither King Manuel, who succeeded Dom Joao, nor Vasco da Gama, the leader of the expedition, had any ambition in this direction. Vasco, in fact, had such crude notions that he mistook a Hindu temple of Kāli to be a Christian church and worshipped there with all solemnity.[1] Europe knew only Islam as a religion different from Christianity. The idol of Kāli was mistaken for a representation of the Virgin, and, though the service must have appeared curious,

1) Faria y Sousa, p. 46.

nothing therein excited his suspicion. Cabral's instructions were based on the assumption that the inhabitants of India were a sort of primitive Christians and that they only wanted instruction to become Romans in their methods of worship.[1] Cabral's fleet contained 8 Franciscan friars, 8 chaplains and a chaplain major. Faria mentions that at Cannanore Cabral knew of the existence of some Christians of St. Thomas under Armenian Bishops.[2] Two Christians from Cranganore, Joseph and Mathew, approached Cabral with a request to take them to Europe, and gave a description of their customs to him. Both of them were taken to Lisbon and educated in the Catholic Faith. Mathew died in Lisbon. Joseph travelled to Venice, Rome and other places, wrote his impressions of those countries and published them in the form of a book entitled "The Travels of Joseph the Indian." Vasco da Gama received messages from Christians in Cranganore who sent a deputation to him asking him to take them under the protection of Portugal.[3]

The Christians of the Syrian Church had been treated generously by Hindu Rulers who had allowed them to live without molestation or interference. Even Gouvea, the biographer of de Meneses, states, "that their privileges were most religiously guarded by native Rajahs." They lived in religious matters under their own *Metrans*. And yet, though the Hindu Rulers had treated them like this, at the very first opportunity,

1) Castenheda III. 130.
2) Faria p. 59.
3) Faria p. 67.

they hastened to disclaim their allegiance and to accept the sovereignty of the King of Portugal. Little did they imagine that by this change they were inviting on themselves a reign of religious terror and oppression which was to culminate in the Synod of Diamper. The centuries of schism and split, which have weakened the ancient and prosperous Church of Malabar may be traced to the foolish and short-sighted action by which its representatives accepted the authority of Portugal. "Kerala Pazhama" gives detailed information[1] about their visit to Gama, which account is also corroborated by Faria.[2] They surrendered their privileges and authority to Portugal and undertook to conduct their affairs only in the name of the Portuguese King. The ancient records and insignia which their Chief possessed were also handed over to Gama. More than even this, they suggested to him that with their help he should conquer the Hindu Kingdoms and invited him to build a fortress for this purpose in Cranganore. This was the recompense which the Hindu Rajahs received for treating with liberality and kindness the Christians in their midst.

The Portuguese policy towards the Christians developed with their increasing authority. The newly converted Christians in Cochin and Quilon were declared to be under the judicial protection of the Portuguese. In all quarrels between a new Christian and a local inhabitant the former was to be handed over to the Portuguese.[3] The main controversy with the Queen of Quilon was about the privileged treat-

1) Kerala Pazhama p. 24. 2) Faria pp. 33 and 61 3) Faria p. 61.

ment, which the Portuguese insisted, should be meted out to the Christians.[1] Under Albuquerque a new policy was initiated of expelling non-Christians from within the walls of Portuguese fortresses. This order led to a number of conversions in Cochin and in Cranganore.

During the life-time of King Manuel the policy of conversion was not dictated by any religious zeal. Its purpose was merely to strengthen the Portuguese hold on the coast. But in the time of Joao III, evangelisation was taken up as a main object of policy. A Bishopric at Goa was created in 1538 and Frei Joao d'Albuquerque, a cousin of the great Governor, was sent out as Bishop. Cochin was soon raised to a Bishopric, and the Malabar coast was placed under it. The King was particularly anxious about the spread of Christianity and wrote to the Viceroy Joao de Castro demanding that all the power of the Portuguese should be directed to this purpose. "The great concernment which lies upon Christian princes to look to matters of Faith and to employ their forces for its preservation makes me advise you how sensible I am that not only in many parts of India under our subjection but in our city of Goa, idols are worshipped, places in which our Faith may be more reasonably expected to flourish; and being well informed with how much liberty they celebrated heathenish festivals

1) Over the St. Thomas or "Syrian" Christians the Portuguese exercised no authority. Moens in his Memorial says, "The company has never had any authority nor could have over St. Thomas Christians who were always subjects of the country princes. Not even the Portuguese exercised any jurisdiction over them." Memorial p. 180.

We command you to discover by diligent officers all the idols and to demolish and break them up in pieces where they are found, proclaiming severe punishments against any one who shall dare to work, cast, make in sculpture, engrave, paint or bring to light any figure of an idol in metal, brass, wood, plaster or any other matter, or bring them from other places; and against who publicly or privately celebrate any of their sports, keep by them any heathenish frankincense or assist and hide the Brahmins, the sworn enemies of the Christian profession . . . It is our pleasure that you punish them with that severity of the law without admitting any appeal or dispensation in the least."[1] As the Portuguese had no territorial possessions in Malabar, except within their fortress walls, this inhuman policy had only an indirect effect. The Governor was instructed to try and convert the Rajah of Cochin who, however, was not so pliant in this matter as in others. The cunning Rajah of Tanur more than once offered to become a Christian, and in fact was formally baptised at Goa, but on his return he kept up his old customs and denied the conversion. But even in Cochin, Cannanore and Quilon none but Christians were allowed to live within the fortress. In 1567 it was decided by the ecclesiastical council, that no Christian was to engage infidel doctors or even be shaved by an infidel barber.

The policy of conversion was naturally unsuccessful in Malabar, where the population was under the

1) Jacinto Frere Andrade. "Life of Dom Joao Casho." Translated into English by Sir Peter Wyche 1664. p. 45.

rule of Hindu Rajahs. The narrow spirit of intolerance which animated the Portuguese was, therefore, felt more by the native Christians than by the Hindu population. The Portuguese Christians always looked upon the local Christians as heretics. Antonio de Gouvea, the enthusiastic historian of Archbishop Meneses, writing in 1609, thus states the attitude of the Catholic Church. "Voila, certes le piteux etat de ces peoples, viola le Chrestiens de St. Thomas, plongez es profondes tenebres et erreurs des le jour que l'eglise de Babylone, leur presenta le hauage plein de poison nestorien et a dure jusques a l'a notre seigneur 1599; quand le seigneur Frere Alexis de Meneses les ramena au gyron de leur mere la sainte eglise Catholique."[1] As soon as an ecclesiastical policy was clearly developed by the establishment of the Archiepiscopal See of Goa with a Bishopric in Cochin, and with the foundation of monastic Orders, an attempt was made to make the Syrian Christians conform to Roman practices. The first attempt was made by the Franciscans who founded a college at Cranganore in 1545 for the education of priests. The Kathanars, or Syrian priests who were trained and ordained by them, were, however, disowned by the Syrians. The Syrian Church in Malabar was administered by *Metrans* or Bishops sent out from Bussorah. Their influence was strong enough to resist Catholic aggression, and, as a result, in 1558 the Portuguese authorities issued an order that foreign ecclesiastics should not be allowed

1) "Histoire Orientale des grands progres de l'eglise Catholique." Anvers 1609, p. 29.

to enter Malabar. On the failure of this attempt the matter was again taken up by the Society of Jesus. They established a college at Vaipukotta in 1587. Instruction in this college, of which the first Principal was Antonio Morales, was given in the Syrian language. But, in spite of this concession, the attempt met with but indifferent success, and, till the time of Alexis de Meneses, the Syrian Christian community continued to be self-governing in internal matters.

In Alexis de Meneses, Archbishop of Goa, Rome had an agent suitable in every way for great political and ecclesiastical missions. Born of the highest nobility, a relation of Kings, able to defy Governments when necessary and to use them when expedient, trained alike to the methods of diplomacy as of force, de Meneses was of the type of priest-politicians whom the Holy See has produced at all times, from Hildebrand to Antonelli. Moreover, de Meneses was intensely religious. He came out as the Archbishop of Goa with no other idea than the spiritual conquest of India and the extension of the powers of the Holy See. Clement VIII in a special Brief asked him to enquire into the state of the Malabar Churches. Like most men of his time, what seemed imperative to him was the "reclamation" of the heretic Christians rather than the conversion of the heathens. With single-minded zeal he set himself immediately to the task of bringing under Rome the Syrian Churches in Malabar. With this object he landed in Cochin on the 26th of January 1599. Arriving at the time when the siege of Kottakkal was going on, de Meneses's first business was diplomatic rather than ecclesiastical. He had to persuade the King of Cochin not to attack a feudatory of the Zamorin during the siege. After he was successful in that mission, de Meneses elaborated his plans for bringing the Malabar Christians within the Church. This could only be done by a regularly constituted Synod, at which, however, it was impossible to get a majority for surrender to Rome, as the native Christians were very tenacious of their Beliefs. Moreover the "Syrian" Christians had found a leader of equal capacity in their Archdeacon who successfully resisted the spiritual and temporal blandishments of the Roman Church and kept his flock in allegiance to their ancient form of worship. Meneses called upon the Archdeacon to come to Cochin and submit to his authority. The Archdeacon had already applied to Bussorah for a Bishop and he was expecting a Syrian Prelate to reach Malabar in time to take up the fight. But the Bishop did not arrive on the fixed date. The Archdeacon rose to the occasion; he refused to recognise the Roman Church; and a Synod which he called at Angamali swore along with the Kathanars to uphold the traditions of the Church without any change and not to accept any Bishop but the one sent out by the Patriarch. It was also agreed that Catholic clergymen should not be allowed to say Mass in Syrian Churches, and that the Kathanars trained at the colleges at Vaipukotta should not be allowed to enter native churches.

De Meneses was furious. He denounced the Archdeacon as a traitor and heretic, and decided upon immediate action against him.

He suggested to the Rajah of Cochin that he should arrest the Archdeacon and hand him over to the Portuguese authorities. As the Rajah would not agree to this, the Archbishop pressed him to use all his temporal authority to make the Christian community bend to the wishes of Rome. After some hesitation the Rajah of Cochin agreed. He did so on the promise that de Meneses would intervene on his behalf for the continuation of certain annual gifts of money which the Portuguese used to make to him but which had been stopped. After this agreement, the minister of the Rajah went along with the Archbishop and announced in all churches that it was the desire of the Ruler that they should obey the orders of Rome.

Armed thus with the temporal authority of the heathen King, whose good offices he did not disdain to use in coercing the Christians, de Meneses went from church to church and used all possible methods to get the St. Thomas Church to accept the supremacy of Rome. A great Synod was held in 1599 for this purpose at Diamper (Udaimperoor) in one of the historical churches of the Christian community of Malabar, and de Meneses carried the day. But his success was only partial. A section of the Syrian Church refused to abide by the decisions of the Synod and continued in its allegiance to Antioch. This was the first of the great schisms in the Malabar Church.

The Church rivalled the State in authority and wealth in the affairs of the Portuguese. The Archbishops and Bishops lived in great magnificence. The property of the churches and the Orders, and the revenue which the State, itself, allowed to them were out of all proportion to the wealth of Portuguese India. Though the Religious Orders, as well as the Church, had large revenues of their own, the State continued to support them. There was levied from the early days of Portuguese establishment in India a one per cent tax for the support of the clergy. The number of the clergy was far in excess of the number of laymen, especially as a large proportion of soldiers, who came out from Portugal, on landing in India joined one of the Orders, because they were not entitled to receive their own pay till after one year of service. The expenditure on ecclesiastics had become a scandal as early as 1550. In 1552 Botelho, writing to King Joao III, the most zealous of all Christian Kings, stated: "The religious in this country desire to spend so freely and give so many alms at the expense of Your revenues that a large part of it goes in this. .... A great part of the revenue is thus alienated."[1]

In 1681, the Viceroy wrote that in certain areas in Travancore the Jesuits had become masters, that they did not obey his orders and that they had usurped Royal authority and jurisdiction.

Cochin was the seat of a Bishopric. Besides a large Cathedral, there were in that city monasteries of the Society of Jesus, of the Franciscans, of the Dominicans, a monastery of Augustine Monks and another of St. Pauls. There was also an ecclesiastical college. At Quilon, besides the famous Church of St. Thomas which was the cause of much quarrel, "there was a

1) "Botelho's cartas," p. 35.

misericordia and a hospital, and the Church was represented by a Vicar-General with two religious Houses, one of St. Francis and one of the Company of Jesus."[1] In every little fort the Church flourished similarly, but at the expense of the State.

The overbearing attitude of the ecclesiastics towards the administration was a matter of complaint from the very beginning. Alone of all the Governors, Albuquerque refused to bow to their pretensions and in fact carried matters with a high hand against the priests. An incident which happened at Cannanore when he was Governor illustrates both the extreme pretensions of the priests and Albuquerque's own attitude towards them. A native Christian who had killed a Hindu had taken sanctuary in a church. Albuquerque ordered the captain, Diogo Correa, to hand him over to the Rajah, which was done. When Albuquerque left Cannanore, the priest fined the captain a heavy sum and placed the whole of Cannanore under an interdict for the high crime of obeying the Governor. Albuquerque was furious that Correa did not take stern measures against the priest and, as a disciplinary action, dismissed that unfortunate man.

One important fact remains to be noticed with regard to the religious policy of the Portuguese. That is the missionary work of St. Francis Xavier.

Francis Xavier, the youngest son of a Spanish gentleman, was born in 1505 in the hilly tracts of the Pyrenees. The name of his family came from his mother, the heiress of the Houses of Azpilqueta and

1) "Noticias da India." p. 235.

Xavier. His father, Juan de Jasso, was high in the employment of the King of Arragon. One of his sisters, Maddelena, who also held a post at the court of Queen Isabella, became later on the famous Abbess of the Poor Clares at Gandia. Very early in life he began to show signs of extreme religiousness and devotion to the Church. He was sent to the Paris University for study where he made the acquaintance of Pierre Lefevre. After completing his studies, Francis became a lecturer on the logic and metaphysics of Aristotle. It was while thus employed that he came under the influence of Ignatius Loyola. He and Lefevre were among the first six who, along with Ignatius, founded the Society of Jesus. It was by chance that Xavier came to be sent out to India. When Joao III asked Ignatius to suggest two members of his Society for missionary work in India the choice first fell on Simon Rodrigues and Bobadilla. But Bobadilla fell ill, and, in his place, Ignatius nominated Xavier.[1] After receiving the blessings of the Pope on the 15th of March 1540, Xavier left Rome with no other provision than his breviary. He reached India early next year and began a remarkable career of evangelisation. After a short time in Goa, he turned his attention to the Malabar Coast; and his main work in India was accomplished among the fisherfolk and other low-caste people of Travancore. In a letter written to the "Brethren of the Society of Jesus" dated January 1544 he describes his method of work among the untouchables, which was somewhat in

1) "Life and Letters of St. Francis Xavier." H. J. Coleridge (S. J.) London, Burns & Oats, 1812, 2 vols. 1 Vol. p. 58.

this manner—"When I first came, I asked them if they knew anything of our Lord Jesus Christ. They only replied that they were Christians and that as they were ignorant of Portuguese they know nothing about the precepts and mysteries of our holy religion. We could not understand one another as I spoke Castilian and they spoke Malabar. So I picked out the most intelligent and well-read of them and then sought out with the greatest diligence men who knew both languages. We held meetings for several days. By our joint efforts and with infinite difficulty we translated the Catechism to the Malabar tongue. This I learnt by heart and then I began to go through all the villages of the coast, calling around me by the sound of a bell as many as I could, children and men. I assembled them twice a day and taught them the Christian doctrine; and thus within the space of one month, the children had it well by heart."[1]

His piety, obvious sincerity, simple life and overwhelming faith appealed to the ignorant folk among whom he worked. Considerable success attended his mission, especially in the southern parts of Travancore where large numbers of fishermen and other low caste people are said to have become Christians. Xavier, however, did not stay to consolidate and organise his work, and left Malabar for other fields. After his departure a considerable portion of his flock seems to have returned to their original habits.

Xavier's mission is of interest, because he may be considered to be the first missionary, in our modern

1) "Life and Letters of St. Francis Xavier." H. J. Coleridge (S. J.) London, Burns & Oats, 1812, 1 Vol. p. 151.

sense. He came to preach the Gospel, to give to the Indian world what he considered the true light. His methods were crude, but he showed an appreciation of popular psychology; and his life, spent among foreign people in the service of his Church, not as the member of a powerful community or as Bishop, but as a preacher, is indeed a source of inspiration.

CHAPTER XIII

THE CAUSES OF THE FAILURE OF THE PORTUGUESE

European writers and historians are accustomed to devote considerable space to explain the causes for the downfall of the Portuguese. It is impossible to understand the fall of Portuguese power unless the main characteristics of their hold on the East are understood. It should, first, be kept in mind that the Portuguese had at no time any Empire in India. The extraordinary habit of the Portuguese writers and historians of talking as if the few fortresses they held on the coast constituted India---a superstition which the Portuguese still have---has misled many European writers into the belief that at some earlier time the Portuguese possessed a territorial empire. In fact the Portuguese possess even now the main centres which they possessed in the 16th century, excepting the fortresses of Cochin, Cannanore and Quilon. In Goa alone they possessed a small territory, which they still hold and govern. Their supremacy was entirely on the sea, and their fall was also, therefore, a matter of naval power.

It is, indeed, a matter of some curiosity that the Portuguese should have held undisputed mastery of the sea routes for over a century. But the explanation of it lies in the fact that Egypt, which was the natural rival of any Power claiming authority on the waters of the Arabian Sea, had been reduced to a province of the Ottoman Empire. The Ottoman naval policy was at no time directed to a maintenance of supremacy on Indian waters. The orientation of Turkish policy under Suleiman the Magnificent was towards the Western Mediterranean. The Turkish admirals were fighting in order to establish their supremacy in Crete, and, under Khair-ed-din Barbarossa, they were menacing the very shores of Italy and Sicily. It is curious that, at the time when the Portuguese supremacy in the Indian Ocean was unquestioned, Barbarossa was making the Turkish name a by-word for terror to the coastal population of the Mediterranean. The European ambitions of Turkey made her neglect the question of the Indian Seas after one or two sporadic attempts. It was this alone that gave the Portuguese their power on the sea. When another nation, equally well equipped like the Dutch, challenged their power, it fell to the ground like a house of cards. As against the smaller Indian coastal Powers they were able to maintain their maritime pretensions; but against the Dutch and the English they were powerless.

We have shown that, so far as administration was concerned, the Portuguese in India developed nothing in the nature of an efficient system. From the earliest times, they showed themselves to be corrupt, inefficient and altogether unfit for the arts of government. The Portuguese soldiers were certainly brave and cared little for life. Some of their leaders were chivalrous and honourable men; but few are the names in

Portuguese Indian history that could add to the military glory of Portugal. Duarte Pacheco and Affonso Albuquerque are the only two names who could bear comparison with men like Bussy or Dupleix, Clive or Goddard. Indeed, but for the pompous exaggerations of her historians, the hundred and fifty years of Indian monopoly, which Portugal enjoyed, pregnant as it is with future history, would have been considered hardly more than an unimportant incident in the history of India.

The connection of the Portuguese with India was mainly a question of trade. What Almeida and Albuquerque desired was to turn to Portugal the whole commercial wealth of India. "The volume of Indian trade is enormous; silks, brocades, copper, mercury, coral etc.; it is almost beyond belief" wrote Albuquerque. It is characteristic, therefore, of the Portuguese relations with India that, while their political prestige diminished and their fortresses and factories were defenceless, the trade continued to increase. The largest commercial fleets that sailed to India were sent after Philip II of Spain had become also the King of Portugal. Till the very end of the Portuguese maritime supremacy the commercial value of the Indian connection kept on rising. But it is at the same time true that the administration itself was never properly solvent. The Governors were always in lack of funds. From the time of Martim de Sousa the Government had taken to the disastrous policy of debasing the coinage. In its final stages the administration permitted dues to be paid in in copper, even accepting in certain ports Chinese copper. The reason for this was that copper was useful for casting cannon; and as the fortresses were left without guns this was the only method of improvising a defence.

From the very beginning, the officers had no other object but private gain. Cosmo Annes, in a letter dated 30th December 1549, had complained that things were going from bad to worse in Cochin. A letter of Alvaro de Mendonco to the King, dated January 8th 1540, declared that the conduct of the Viceroy was so corrupt that "no one could remain here who could have a loophole for departing." The only object of the officials was to enrich themselves either by peculation or by private trade.

Officers were not regularly paid. In fact, till the time of Joao de Castro, the pay was not fixed. Even when there was a nominal salary, often it was not forthcoming. Garcia de Noronha neglected to pay the salaries of the officers; and it was not uncommon that payment was long in arrears. For Indian service salary was of course the least consideration. A system of *percaloes* or profits was attached to each office, which brought to the holder enormous sums. The pay and *profits* of each appointment were calculated with great care in 1612 by Figuere de Falcao, and this document, which may still be examined in Lisbon, gives remarkable figures. One minor captaincy, the pay of which for three years did not come up to £1,000, brought a profit of £57,000 to the holder. When the authorities in Portugal came to know of the enormous profits attached to these offices, it seemed to them to be a royal and easy way to enrich the coffers of the State. The King ordered that all these appointments should be put up for auction and sold to the highest bidder—surely a singular way of carrying on Government.[1]

This was not all. The ruling authorities in Lisbon developed the custom of sending out to India orphan girls, with patents of Indian appointments as dowry. No doubt, in modern States also, the system of providing public offices to those who undertake the obliging duty of marrying well-placed women is not quite unknown. But the Portuguese government had no qualms about it. Offices were given openly as dowries; and one lady brought with her out to India the King's order of appointment for the captaincy of Cranganore to any one who cared to marry her. Matters went so far, that the Viceroy had to represent that this procedure would lessen the revenue which the State received by auctioning the appointments; and in accordance with his representation a law was made whereby offices given as dowry were valid only for three years.

Nepotism was another vice among the Portuguese authorities. The Governors and their officers brought out to India their sons and nephews and placed them in all the offices of advantage, and protected them in their career of peculation. Gaspar Gonsalvo, writing early in the 16th century during the Governorship of Lope Soares, represented the matter to the King thus: "Your Highness should not send out as Captain-in-Chief nor as factor, nor as one for your treasury any who has a son or relative or any near relatives. Your High-

1) Facisculo 6. "Archivo Portuguez Oriental" No. 353. P. 1059.

ness should be particularly careful about the factor who comes out to Cochin, because the factory of Cochin is the largest house that King or Prince ever had and therefore it needs a man of great sufficiency."[1] Unfortunately this excellent piece of advice was never taken.

It can be imagined what utter demoralisation would characterise an administration based on these principles. There was no honesty in public services, no discipline in the army and no loyalty towards each other. "Robbery," wrote St. Francis Xavier, "is so public and common, that it hurts no one's character and is hardly counted as a fault." As for discipline, there are some most extraordinary cases recorded. In 1539, a company of soldiers, taking possession of a fortress in Diu, turned their guns on their countrymen. Nothing was done to them, though a later Viceroy wrote to the King that he "would have seen them dead and the site of the fortress sown with salt."[2]

No nation with an administration so corrupt and based on principles so unwholesome could conquer a country; and, in spite of popular belief to the contrary, India was never an easy country to conquer. The British, with much greater naval, military and economic power, and an organisation which was the model of all imperial governments, took 100 years to conquer India. From their first intervention in Arcot to the annexation of the Punjab, there is a century of unceasing warfare, in which the superior organisation

1) "Gavitas Antigas". Maco 6. Document No. 81.

2) Letter October 30, 1540, of Joao Castro, Investigator Portuguez.

and military equipment of the British finally gained for them the Empire of India. And the British were favoured by the circumstance that, at the time they stood forth as an Indian Power bidding for supremacy in the land, India was divided and disorganised as a result of the decay of Mogul power. The Portuguese never had, and never could have had, anything like an empire, or even the shadow of a territorial power in India. Established in Goa, Daman, Diu and Cochin, they controlled the sea trade. But on land they were powerless. The Zamorin drove them out of Chaliyam. The minor princes, whose territories lay beyond the range of their ships' guns, defied them. In fact, Portuguese India is a myth. One might as well talk of Abyssinian India, because the little town of Jinjira was held by an Abyssinian family. It is merely the pompous boast of Portuguese historians that have conveyed to Europe generally the impression that the Portuguese were in some way the masters of India. There is a Portuguese "Governor General" for the few square miles marked Portuguese on the map, and still that territory is officially called India, or the Estado da India. Historical foolishness and meaningless pretensions could go no further. The Portuguese never lost India, because they never possessed it; they never came anywhere near to possessing it. Their's was merely a supremacy on the sea gained by purely adventitious circumstances, which vanished with the arrival in Indian waters of the Dutch and the British.

CHAPTER XIV

MALABAR AT THE END OF THE PORTUGUESE PERIOD

The Portuguese relations with Malabar lasted for over a period of 150 years. Politically, economically and socially, the adventurers who followed Vasco da Gama represented a type different from those to which Malabar was accustomed. Their arrival on the scene had undeniable effects on the whole life of Malabar. It changed the course of Malabar history, introduced new factors in its economic life, and materially altered the social conditions. A survey of Malabar at the time that the Dutch drove the Portuguese out of Malabar waters would show the extent of the change which their influence had brought about.

Politically the most important result of the Portuguese establishment in Malabar was that it checked the development of Malabar into a single confederacy under the Zamorin. The whole history of the 160 years, from the establishment of a factory by Cabral at Cochin to the capture of that fort by Van Goens, may be summarised from the point of view of Malabar as a successful attempt by the Rajah of Cochin, with the help of the Portuguese, to stem the tide of the expanding power of the Zamorin. Cochin was reduced to an absolute dependency of Portugal. But, while the Cochin Rajah grew powerless as against the

Portuguese Captain who could at any moment reduce his palace to ashes, he became a powerful Ruler as against the princes and Chieftains of the interior. From a local Chief of no importance, the Cochin Rajah, with the help of the Portuguese, rose to the position of a powerful prince, independent of the Zamorin and a rival to him in the claim of allegiance of the southern princes.

Besides this, the growth of royal power, which was a development of significance, also met with a decisive check. The policy of the Portuguese was to deal directly with the small princes and Chiefs and to conciliate them by money gifts. They made alliances with princes, like the Rajah of Tanur who was a feudatory of the Zamorin, and the Rajah of Procaud over whom the Ruler of Cochin claimed authority. By this method the Portuguese were able to safeguard their commercial interests, and at the same time see that no Malabar Ruler became powerful enough to drive them out of Cochin or Cannanore. During the 150 years of Portuguese connection the power of the smaller Chiefs continued to increase at the expense of the larger Rajahs. The Rulers of coastal tracts became powerful, and began to question the authority of the suzerains, knowing well that in any contest they could get the support of the Portuguese if they could pay for it. The Chiefs who rose to power as a result of this policy were the Rajahs of Procaud, Mangat, Parur, Quilon and Tanur. Tanur, especially, played the Portuguese against the Zamorin and the Zamorin against the Portuguese, and by this means came to occupy an important position in the history of Malabar. It will be remembered that the fortress of Chaliyam was sold to the Portuguese by this Ruler; that he even went so far as Goa, proclaiming loudly that he wanted to be converted, and that on his return, after all these pretensions of goodwill, quietly marched with the Zamorin to Vaduthalai to fight against the Portuguese. The increased power of the smaller Chiefs was a direct result of the decisive check to the growth of the Zamorin's royal power. It put back the clock of Malabar history by 200 years, and perpetuated the division of the country into small principalities, each jealous of its neighbour and carrying on interminable feuds with others. It was this state of political disunion, which the Dutch took great care to foster, that made Malabar an easy prey for Haider Ali.

Economically, Malabar underwent even greater changes. The Portuguese introduced into Malabar a number of new products such as the Kishu tree—still known in Malabar as the Feringhee tree. They introduced tobacco and its cultivation. But, more than all, they created a world market for Malabar products. At the time of the Moorish trade Malabar spices were a delicacy which made a strong but not a very large appeal. The direct exportation of pepper, cardamom, cinnamon, ginger, and other Malabar produce into Europe created a great demand for them. In the course of a few years the economic situation of the country had altered as a result of this ever-increasing demand. Orta mentions that "pepper was grown from Cape Comorin to Cannanore. In Malabar it is largely consumed in the country itself. A large quantity goes to the Red Sea against the orders of the King but nothing can be so well guarded but that much will be taken westward by the Moors. Though there are some trees to the north of Cannanore they are so few that we do not take account of them." Almost every acre of ground capable of growing pepper and ginger was cultivated; and the trade which, before this time was mainly in the hands of a few big merchants, became a business of the people at large. People were quick to appreciate the changed position. The Moors had merely bought what had been produced in the country. The Portuguese were anxious to get as much as could be produced, and even put pressure on Chiefs and Rulers to encourage pepper and ginger cultivation.

The Portuguese contact also introduced great changes in the cultivation of cocoanut. It would seem that cocoanut was not one of the major products of Malabar before the Portuguese came. *Unninili Sandesam*, which describes the trade of Kayamkulam, Quilon and other ports and mentions many different kinds of rice sold, does not mention cocoanuts even once as a commodity of export. For household and local uses cocoanut was grown; but there was nothing like a cultivation for purposes of trade. It was only in 1503 that the Portuguese learnt, from one of the prize ships taken off Curia Muria Islands, the use of coir as ropes for their ships. From that time coir became an important article of trade, and more for coir than for Copra, cocoanut cultivation became popular. Orta says of coir in his colloquies: "Of it they make the riggings and cordage for all ships. It is very serviceable for us, for it is very flexible and does not rot in salt water. All the ships are caulked with it so that it serves as linen as oakum and as matting. These qualities make it good merchandise for Portugal."[1] To this day, coir is one of the chief exports of Malabar. Even in cocoanut trade the Portuguese connection with Africa was of help to Malabar. Seed nuts of a better and bigger type of cocoanut were introduced into Malabar by them and are even now called *Kappal thenga* or cocoanuts from the ships. As cocoanut cultivation was particularly suited to the coastal tracts of Malabar, it soon became one of the chief products of the country. It is stated that at Cannanore, in 1564 Dom Payo de Noronha cut down no less than 40,000 cocoanut trees as an act of terrorism.

The Portuguese had put a stop to the historic commercial connection between Malabar, Arabia and Egypt. In its place the new European trade had grown up, bringing more money and luxury into the country. The trade was more widespread, and the resulting prosperity was also not confined to ports or small communities but to the whole people. The construction of houses on European models became fashionable; and we are informed that at Cochin, Calicut, Quilon and other places there were many stately buildings. Money was plentiful; and the system of cash payments to Rulers, by which the Portuguese kept them in good humour, tended to the growth of greater luxury.

1) Orta "Colloquies" Page 141. Translation by Markham, London Southern & Co. MCMXII.

More than all this, the old methods of Malabar warfare underwent great change. Firearms became common and helped to increase the power of the Chiefs and Rajahs. Fortifications were undertaken in a more systematic manner—both the Zamorin and the Rajah of Cannanore had trained artillery men in their service.

A hundred and fifty years of Portuguese trade had seen the growth of many new towns and the decay of old ones. Calicut continued to be the most important town on the West Coast; but Cochin, which had come into existence as the result of a great flood in 1341 and was only an unimportant village when Cabral arrived there, had risen to the position of a very important commercial centre. Its public buildings were imposing structures, and the fortress, rebuilt by Albuquerque, was one of the strongest in India. Cæsar Frederick, who visited India between 1563 and 1581 described Cochin as "the chiefest place that the Portugals have in the Indies next unto Goa."[1] Baldeus mentions that the Jesuit Church and College facing the seashore had a lofty steeple......The College was three stories high. Cæsar Frederick also mentions "that the Jesuit Church which was magnificently built of square stones exceeded all the rest in height and beauty." The Augustin Friars, Franciscans and Jesuits had likewise their several convents magnificently built with very pleasant gardens and walks. Captain Nieuhoff, himself, states that the Portuguese had beautified the city with many fine edifices, churches and monasteries. "In the suburbs towards the landside were several goodly

1) "Hakluyts' voyages." Vol. V. pp. 392-395.

churches, and a little nearer the seashore was the monastery of St. John. Here the Austin Friars, Franciscans and Jesuits had likewise their several convents, all magnificently built with very pleasant gardens and walks. Among other steeples that of St. Paul, being magnificently built of square stones, excelled all the rest in height and beauty which is since demolished with all the other churches except one."[1] The growth of Cochin was entirely the result of Portuguese trade, and its importance dates only from the visit of Cabral.

Other towns which grew into importance were Chaliyam, where the Portuguese erected a fortress but from which they were driven out in 1570; Pudapattanam, which was founded by the Kunjalis as their capital, and Procaud, the Rajah of which became an important Chief only after his alliance with the Portuguese. But the older towns of Quilon and Cranganore lost a great deal of their importance. Cranganore, especially, became a cockpit of warfare between the Zamorin and the Portuguese, and its traditional greatness, dating back many centuries before Christ, vanished during this period.

Portuguese influence in matters of education is also worthy of notice. The colleges founded at Angamali and Cochin for the education of Malabar Christians in the Roman Faith were useful in spreading the knowledge of Latin and Portuguese. The later Rajahs of Cochin conversed fluently in Portuguese, and often corresponded directly in that language. In fact, till the establishment of British supremacy in Malabar

1) "Nieuhoff's voyages." p. 221.

Portuguese continued to be the diplomatic language of the Malabar Rulers. For instance, all the letters addressed by the Zamorin to the English factor, for over half a century after the disappearance of the Portuguese from Malabar, were written in the language of Cameons.

For their own commercial and political purposes the Portuguese were forced to learn Malayalam; and the list of Malabar words at the end of the Rotiero may be said to be the forerunner of oriental research by Europeans. Francis Xavier's translation of the Catechism into Malayalam is the crude beginning of the new movement of translation from western languages which has become so marked a feature of Indian vernaculars to-day. The descriptions of Malabar left by Duarte Barbosa, Gaspar Correa and the historians must also be counted among the benefits which have resulted from the relations between Portugal and Malabar.

An influential school of history holds that the benefits, that India has received from the direct contact with Europe, are of such a nature that, in spite of all their faults, the Portuguese should be considered as the pioneers of civilisation and as the forerunners of the British Empire. It may be permitted however, to question the correctness of the point of view, wrongly called historical, which thus tries to import retrospective values into events of an earlier date. Even accepting that the connection with Europe has been beneficial to India, it is open to doubt whether a century and a half of barbarous outrages, of unscrupulous plunder and of barren aggression, is not too great a price to pay for the doubtful benefits of having the way opened for other European traders. India's own direct trade was ruined, and, in its place, there was established a monopoly by alien races, which had the effect of draining the wealth of India into Europe. The Portuguese could not even claim what the Mahommedan Rulers of India could legitimately put forward in their justification, that they had a cultural contribution to make to the life of India, such as we may, even now, see in the magnificent architectural monuments at Agra, Delhi, Ahmedabad. The Portuguese of the 16th and the 17th centuries had nothing to teach the people of India except improved methods of killing people in war and the narrow feeling of bigotry in religion. Surely, these were not matters of such importance as to make it necessary for Indians to feel grateful towards Vasco da Gama or his successors. The relations between Portugal and India were barren of cultural or political results, and there is in that history nothing which any civilised nation can be proud of. A host of imaginative historians, anxious to sing the glory of their fatherland, have pictured to us the heroic story of a small nation going forth to conquer India and holding it under sway for 150 years, fighting and winning battles against great hordes and conquering heathen worlds for Christ. Europe has accepted as true, for too long a time, the myths and legends of Barroes, Castenheda and Correa. The idea is wholly and absolutely untrue. The Portuguese had mastery of the Indian seas; but never had they the mastery of any area in India outside the range of their ships' guns. The battles they won were more mythical than actual; and the pompous descriptions of Portuguese historians should not make us forget that all their campaigns were nothing more than indecisive skirmishes against very minor local Chieftains. It is indeed a fine picture which writers have drawn for us—a small heroic country draining itself of its best blood in a great attempt to conquer and hold India! But the picture has not even a background of truth except in the vainglorious phraseology of the Portuguese Kings, who called their administrative representatives, the "Viceroys of India," and the few square miles of territory at Goa, the "Estado da India."

INDEX